METAL

COFFINS

The Blood Alliance Cartel

MICHAEL S. VIGIL

The Ishmael Tree

NEW YORK   SHARJAH

Michael S. Vigil/The Ishmael Tree
244 Fifth Avenue
New York, New York 10001
www.ishmaeltree.com

Publisher's Note: This is a work of fiction. Names, characters, places, and incidents are a product of the author's imagination. Locales and public names are sometimes used for atmospheric purposes. Any resemblance to actual people, living or dead, or to businesses, companies, events, institutions, or locales is completely coincidental.

Ordering Information:
Quantity sales. Special discounts are available on quantity purchases by corporations, associations, and others. For details, contact the "Special Sales Department" at the address above.

Metal Coffins: The Blood Alliance Cartel/Michael S. Vigil.
ISBN 978-0-9915821-9-8

Dedication

*This book is dedicated to the loving memory
of my parents, Sam and Alice, whose sacrifice, support,
and love made me the person I am today.*

*It is also dedicated to my sisters, Anita and Mona.
To my niece Ursula who is my bright shining star.*

And to Nicole who is in heaven with my parents.

*To my stepdaughter Lisa Haynie and my grandchildren,
Luke Edward and Sarah Claire, who make life a complete
joy.*

*To my loving wife, Suzanne, who takes care of me
and makes me see the beauty of the world.*

*To my great publisher, Gigi Ishmael, whose
invaluable advice, counsel, and support
made this book possible.*

*To Dr. D. McCoy for your advice and editing,
which was instrumental to my book.*

*To my friend, Alvan Romero, retired IRS Special Agent,
who provided phenomenal support in the editing of Metal
Coffins.*

FOREWORD

I am truly honored to contribute the foreword for this fascinating book by retired Drug Enforcement Administration (DEA) Special Agent, Michael S. Vigil primarily for three reasons. First, I have known and greatly admired Michael for over 25 years. Second, I had the privilege to work directly for Mr. Vigil while he was the Special Agent in Charge (SAC) of the Caribbean Field Division of the DEA. Very few DEA special agents are promoted to the Senior Executive Service (SES) rank (less than one percent of the agent population) and not all of them become SACs. Michael Vigil was the SAC of two major DEA Field Divisions and he was also the Chief of International Operations where he led global enforcement, operations, intelligence, and money laundering initiatives. Third, this book, like his last one, is captivating and difficult to put down.

Although fiction, but based on true events, this absorbing book provides a riveting account of the complex world of structured criminal organizations with layered networks of illicit drug manufacturers, wholesale buyers and sellers, facilitators, middlemen, hitmen and enforcers, and retail level distributors. The book covers the inevitable corruption, coercion and intimidation of some; the commitment, courage and resolve of others, and the horrific violence and incredible danger faced by everyone associated with transnational organized crime and drug law enforcement. This fast-action book graphically describes the *Danger, Excitement and Adventure* that is the DEA and is written by one of its most celebrated special agents.

I first met Mr. Vigil in 1990, when I was a special agent assigned to the DEA Nassau Bahamas Country Office. The Nassau Country Office reported to the DEA Miami Field Division, which is second only to the DEA New York Field Division in size. Mr. Vigil, who led an enforcement group in the Miami Field Division, was widely known as the most aggressive and tenacious supervisory special agent in the Division. His enforcement group was number one in everything; arrests, seizures, investigations, informants, intelligence collection; you name it they were first.

I travelled to the Miami Field Division from the Bahamas to meet with Mr. Vigil and his agents to coordinate and discuss how we could best proceed on an investigation I had been working in Nassau that was connected to their case. Soon after I began to describe my investigation, I was politely but firmly told that Mr. Vigil had already decided they had much better evidence and my investigation would support theirs. It was a short meeting and given Mr. Vigil's reputation and his "hospitality," I quickly agreed to proceed with the investigation in the manner suggested, my investigation would support theirs. That was the beginning of my association with Mr. Vigil who became Mike in 2003 upon my promotion to the SES rank, however I still find myself fondly calling him "Jefe" (Spanish for boss) and referring to him as "The Boss."

As I read this book, I remembered and thought about how Mr. Vigil through his affable, outgoing but firm personality, comprehensive knowledge of transnational organized crime, extensive drug law enforcement experience, confidence, determination and sheer will would inspire others to join him and work collaboratively on an investigation. In 1992, while assigned to Freeport, Bahamas, I traveled to Buenos Aires, Argentina to take part in the annual International Drug Enforcement Conference (IDEC) and had the good fortune to observe Mr. Vigil skillfully interact and connect with our foreign counterparts from all over the world.

During the 1992 conference, I spent a great deal of time with Mr. Vigil for two reasons. First, my Spanish language skills were weak and second, he seemed to know everybody there and he freely shared his vast contacts with me.

I am certain many of the Mexican law enforcement officers I met through Mike Vigil and throughout my career are characters in this spellbinding book. I know you are going to enjoy meeting some of these officers more than others as you acquire a deeper understanding of the magnitude of the illicit drug trade and its formidable challenge.

William J. Walker
Brigadier General, U.S. Army National Guard
Deputy Assistant Administrator (Retired),
U.S. Drug Enforcement Administration

CHAPTER
1

METAL COFFINS

I t is an early Saturday morning in Mexico City and John Hawkins slowly gets out of bed and opens the heavy curtains of his room at the Maria Isabel Sheraton Hotel. The bright sunlight floods into the room and he peers across the street at the U.S. Embassy with its vast array of antennas on the roof. Despite being closed for the weekend, security is heavy with blue uniformed guards everywhere and wooden barricades that have seen better days seal off the side streets from regular traffic. He hears the incessant sound of frustrated drivers honking their horns and the yells of sidewalk vendors hawking trinkets to gullible tourists on the overly congested Avenida Reforma. He also notices the thick brownish color in the air and mumbles, *"Goddamn pollution is going to kill me."*

Hawkins is a sales representative for a company that sells tractors and other farm equipment to wealthy farmers throughout the country. He makes a good salary, but living out of a suitcase gets old. Hawkins was born in New York City, but his parents decide to move to Tucson, Arizona, when he was six years old because of his chronic asthma. The drier climate definitely alleviates much of his health problem. His Irish genes color his hair red and give him a white, pasty complexion that is almost transparent. He is short, stocky, and has an infectious laugh, especially when he drinks single malt scotch. He often tells friends the Irish would rule the world if not for their love of alcohol.

A couple of months prior to his trip, his wife of ten years divorced him because she wanted to "find herself." Heart-broken, he began to drink a lot more than usual. He refers to it as *therapy through chemistry*. What irritated him was that she started to date a much younger man who looked like a fugitive from a tattoo parlor. She refers to her new boyfriend as *"artistic"* and *"expressive"* through the dozens of tattoos that adorn his arms and face.

Hawkins spitefully tells her, *"He looks like a goddamn ex-convict from a Salvadorian jail."*

That doesn't go over well and ends in a heated shouting match. It quickly escalates, and she chases him to his car with one of his favorite golf clubs and proceeds to viciously attack the hood. The piercing metallic banging comes in quick repetition, leaving scores of large dents and swathes of stripped black paint. Tires squeal wildly in a cloud of burnt rubber as he frantically backs out of the driveway and yells out the window, "You fucking crazy bitch!"

Hawkins finishes his business and decides to take a few days off and drive to Acapulco and enjoy some warm rays from the sun and the soft, white sand at the beach. After having a large breakfast of huevos rancheros and warm tortillas at the hotel café, he loads his bags into the rental SUV. He feels nervous and agitated as he drives past the green Volkswagen Beetle taxicabs and decrepit gray public transportation "peseros" (buses) that whiz by recklessly in complete disregard for the safety of their passengers and other fellow travelers on the road. The local police are out in full force collecting their daily quota of *mordidas* (bribes).

Hawkins sees a police car maneuver next to a white sedan in front of him and is incredulous when money exchanges hands, as both cars are moving no less. He smirks and thinks to himself, "Mexico is truly the land of the triple curse: corruption, conspiracies and cantinas. It seems like an eternity before he gets on the main road to the beach resort. His mind begins to fantasize about the beautiful girls he will undoubtedly meet at the local clubs or at least see them tanning their voluptuous bodies on the beach. Hawkins continues to drive through heavy traffic and the draft from the moving cars swirls road trash high into the air, which is scattered by oncoming cars. The buildings along the road are old and near collapse from decades of neglect, but the people seem impervious or perhaps they just don't care.

About an hour from Mexico City, Hawkins notices a large 55-gallon barrel painted bright blue next to the road.

"What idiot would dump that so close to the highway?" he thinks to himself. A few seconds later, he notices another one covered in red paint.

"I wonder if those barrels accidently fell from a truck?" he whispers to himself as though talking to a phantom passenger. Hawkins travels another half mile and sees a third barrel just a couple of feet from the road. This one is black and doesn't have a lid. He slams on his brakes and pulls onto the narrow shoulder of the highway. Looking through his rear view mirror, he doesn't see any cars approaching and plops down from his SUV with a heavy thud, almost spraining his ankle.

He slowly jogs over to the barrel and notices it is filled with concrete, but then sees something dark sticking out of it. Initially, he thinks it is an animal with thick black fur. As he gets closer, he realizes, to his horror, it is a man's head. The face is frozen in the terror of its last moments on Earth; the eyes are wide and unseeing. The mouth is open and black insects are crawling around in it. Hawkins screams in abject terror and jumps back, stumbling over a large rock. He falls on his back with a loud groan and quickly crawls away from the barrel. He manages to flag down the driver of a cattle truck who parks in front of Hawkins' SUV.

The man, a peasant farmer, with old leather huaraches (sandals) and dirt-encrusted feet walks over to Hawkins, "Señor, estás teniendo problemas con el coche?" (Sir, are you having problems with your car?) He smiles, revealing several missing teeth and the ones that remain are capped in bright silver. Hawkins is still in shock and can't speak. He slowly raises his arm and with his right index finger points at the barrel.

The perplexed farmer saunters cautiously to the barrel and seeing the head, utters, "Dios mio, tenemos que llamar a la policia federal, ellos sabrán qué hacer." (My God, we must call the federal police; they will know what to do.)

A few hours later, Comandante Florentino Ventura of the Mexican Federal Judicial Police (Federales) arrives with seven of his agents in two black Ford sedans with heavily tinted windows. They all have Colt .45's with gold grips decorated with the Mexican eagle clutching a serpent in its beak. The handguns are visibly tucked into the inside of their front waistbands. Ventura is tall with jet-black hair that hangs lazily over his forehead. He wears expensive ostrich cowboy boots and has a large gaudy gold bracelet on his right wrist. A solid gold Rolex watch adorns the other wrist.

He was born and raised in Badiraguato, Sinaloa, a small rural village with nothing to offer other than poverty and misery. Many of the people in the area turned to the trafficking of illegal drugs in order to survive. They grew marijuana in small plots in the mountains and opium poppy from which they extracted opium gum that was sold to major traffickers who converted it into high grade brown or black tar heroin in rustic, isolated conversion labs. These high-powered traffickers had well-established pipelines into the U.S. and numerous distribution cells in every major city that generated hundreds of millions of dollars each year. The peasant farmers were not educated enough to understand the irreparable damage they were doing to humanity. And even if they knew, it is highly unlikely they cared. Ventura is one of the few who isn't enticed to go into the lucrative drug world.

His mother, Imelda, a beautiful, olive skinned woman with dark brown hair and a natural smile, kept him on the straight and narrow and made sure he was devoted to his studies. She would say, *"La educación es tu futuro."* (Education is your future.) She devoted a lot of time and energy keeping him from the clutches of his uncles who were all drug traffickers and wanted their nephew to work with them.

They would tell Ventura, *"No seas tonto! Usted puede hacerse rico vendiendo drogas. Ir a la escuela es para tontos."* (Don't be stupid! You can get rich selling drugs. Going to school is for fools.)

Like most traffickers, Ventura's uncles prefer to work with family members since they can be trusted to keep their mouths shut. To them, blood ties are important to a close knit and effective criminal organization. Even though Ventura stays away from dealing drugs, he killed a man when he was only seventeen years old. He caught a thief trying to steal one of their three horses from the rustic corral behind his house. He shot him with a high-powered rifle leaving a bloody, ragged hole in his chest. It is the law of the sierra and it is brutally swift and lethal.

As a child, Ventura became interested in law enforcement and after graduating from preparatoria (high school) he joined the federal police. It is dangerous work, but he thinks of it as more of an adventure. He is cunning, intelligent and learned to speak fluent English in school, allowing him to rise quickly through the ranks. The rank and file agents admire his courage and toughness. He is not an idealist; his view of the world is more pragmatic. Although, he doesn't take money from traffickers, he accepted money from people who wanted political favors. His conscience is comfortable with arranging meetings with high-ranking politicians or expediting long, bureaucratic processes for people. It is a tradition in Mexico. It enhanced his meager police salary. Ventura knew that life in Mexico is not simply black or white, it is much more complicated and to satisfy even basic needs one had to sometimes stray into the gray areas. Ventura understood this from early childhood. He saw the majority of civil servants seek office, not to serve the public, but to enrich themselves as much as possible during their time in power.

After arriving on the scene, Ventura barks out orders to his men, "Pongan los barriles en el camión para que podamos llevarlos a la oficina y examinarlos y tomar fotos. Tendremos que conseguir algunos martillos y cinceles para recuperar los cuerpos." (Put the barrels on the truck so we can take them to the office and examine them and take photos. We will have to get some hammers and chisels to recover the bodies.)

His men move quickly and commandeer the peasant's truck to collect all of the barrels. The peasant protests, but knows he is wasting his breath. Mexican federal police have the power of life and death so his protests are nothing but whispered grumblings. One of the federales is sent further down the road to see if more barrels can be located, but returns half an hour later and says he had not seen any others. Ventura, prior to leaving the area obtains Hawkins' cell number in the event he has more questions for him later on. Hawkins, in a traumatic haze, slowly drives away; knowing the horrific sight he has just witnessed will be etched in his mind for the rest of his life. He can hardly wait to get to the nearest bar and have several shots of tequila. Hell, maybe the entire bottle. Yes, he would…

On the way back to Mexico City, Ventura calls his friend from the DEA, Miguel Villa, an agent who has been assigned to the U.S. Embassy for almost five years. He tells him to meet him at his office in an hour. Villa is of Hispanic descent and was born and raised in a poor, small village in northern New Mexico. His first language was Spanish and it wasn't until he started elementary school that he learned English. The tough streets in which he was raised prepared him well for the dangerous work that was to come his way as a DEA agent.

As a teenager, he went to school with a lot of pachucos (street thugs) and understood their slang and convoluted thinking. The pachucos were proud to have brothers or relatives in prison. He recalled one of them proudly boasting, *"Yo tengo un carnal en la grande"* that in pachuco jargon meant, "I have a brother in prison." He learned to understand the criminal mind and deviant behavior.

After graduating from high school, Villa attended New Mexico State University located in the southern part of the state and earned a degree in criminology with honors. He struggled the first semester because the high school he attended didn't provide him with the strong foundation required for college studies. He, however, was driven and of the mind-set all obstacles could be overcome with hard work and vision. His parents, like Comandante Ventura's, always preached that an education was synonymous with success. He applied with the Drug Enforcement Administration and was elated when he received a job offer. He had to successfully complete the rigorous training academy and then he would be on probation for a year.

Prior to leaving for the academy in Washington, D.C., he went to one of the local clothing stores to buy a few suits since he didn't own any. The store had a very limited selection so he bought two suits, and two blazers; one was blue and the other bright red. A few equally ostentatious clip-on ties and he was set. Villa breezed through the physical exercises and classroom work to graduate from the academy, which so many others failed. Villa was tall, strongly built, with dark hair and a thick mustache. He also had sleepy eyes that add to his bad boy persona when he worked undercover.

He had an international face allowing him to pass for Italian, Turkish, Central Asian, or Middle Eastern.

The federales all like him because he didn't suffer from the Ugly American Syndrome like so many others who thought they were superior to their neighbors from the south. Villa understood personal relationships were the key to getting things done in Mexico or any foreign assignment for that matter. He broke bread and spent many nights drinking tequila with the feds. For Villa, work against some of the most violent and treacherous drug lords in the world was not an eight to five job. It is a 24/7 effort, but he loved every minute of it. It is the ultimate chess game of life and death where only the most cunning and ruthless minds prevailed. He was addicted to the adrenaline rush only extreme danger generated. He had been involved in many gun battles with drug traffickers and had killed more than he could count in close quarter shootouts. He didn't feel remorse. It was self-defense, pure and simple, he would live or they would live. He lived. He referred to the killings as "social cleansing."

Having similar upbringings, Ventura and Villa became close friends. They trusted each other implicitly and confided in each other. They also learned to be wary of the internal forces within their agencies. Each man understood the shadows of treachery were always hidden within the bureaucracy of their respective organizations. At times, the threat it posed was as dangerous as facing the most devious drug trafficker. Both know they were destined to do great things, but the Grim Reaper was always close by waiting, watching and grinning. He knew the reaper would win in the end. He always won, but for now, they ignored him. They weren't afraid of risks and felt disdain and revulsion for those who simply wanted to play it safe and accomplish nothing of value.

CHAPTER 2

DISMEMBERED BODIES

Villa is already waiting at the offices of the federal police when Ventura and his men arrive and drive into the parking lot with the loud crunching of tires on gravel and the clanging of the barrels as they roll back and forth on the truck. Ventura jumps out of his car with a broad grin and approaches Villa giving him a traditional Mexican abrazo (hug). He then yells orders to his men, telling them to unload the heavy barrels. He also tells one of his agents standing nearby to tell the Ministerio Publico Federal (Federal prosecutor) they have arrived. The short, dark skinned man, dressed in dusty jeans and a red western shirt, smiles broadly revealing several sparkling gold-capped teeth.

He responds, "A sus ordenes, mi comandante." (At your service, my commander) and runs to the nearby building, which houses two federal prosecutors. Mexican law requires that federal prosecutors examine the remains of people either killed by the federal police or homicides investigated by them. They write detailed reports and place them haphazardly in investigative case files. Since they have no standardized filing system, finding the reports later is always grueling.

One of the prosecutors, a tall, gaunt man in his seventies with patches of gray hair, shuffles slowly to Ventura and with a puzzled look inquires, "Qué chingados ha pasado y qué hay en esos barriles?" (What the fuck happened and what is in those barrels?)

Ventura quickly explains the events of the day and tells him that at least one of the barrels contains the remains of a human body. Once the barrels are unceremoniously rolled off the truck, Ventura, Villa, and the prosecutor begin to examine them. A cursory check reveals the name *ChemCon*, Stuttgart, Germany, stamped on the bottom of each barrel. They also have sequential six-digit serial numbers. Villa writes all the information on a small notepad and uses his cell phone to take several photographs. Villa also has latent fingerprints lifted from the barrels even though much of the evidence has already been contaminated. Villa is aware the Mexican police aren't well trained in the identification, collection, and preservation of evidence, which makes investigations in Mexico problematical and difficult to solve.

Six burly agents then begin the arduous task of cutting the barrels open with hammers and chisels. The incessant pounding is deafening, but within minutes they are able to remove the metal casings and then begin to chip away at the dense concrete. This is far more labor intensive and sweat begins to pour from their faces as though they had been doused with buckets of water.

Their shirts are soaked and the gasping for air is heard between grunts of each swing of the heavy hammers. As they remove the cement, body parts begin to appear. The bloody severed heads, arms, legs, torsos, contained in each of the barrels are placed separately on heavy plastic tarps. Villa and Ventura examine the dismembered bodies and both agree a chain saw is the likely instrument used in these grisly murders. They base their theory on the ragged cuts through skin and bone. The bodies also have numerous visible stab wounds, particularly to the chest area. Severe bruises and contusions suggest they had been brutally tortured before they were savagely killed. Clothing is also found as though the killers, on a whim, had decided to throw those in with the bodies.

The clothing is stiff and rough to the touch because they are covered in thick, gray cement. They find miscellaneous items like breath mints, car keys, and pocket change. One pair of pants also contains several condoms. Miraculously, all of the back pockets from the three sets of pants found in the barrels contain wallets and identifications. Villa removes the driver's licenses bearing names and addresses. Also in the wallets were business cards and medical identifications with the names, Dr. Pablo Uribe, Dr. Jaime Montoya, and Dr. Jose Martinez. The business cards all had the same address: Hospital Centro Medico, Rio Magdalena, No. 1001 y Ave. Revolución, Colonia Tizapán San Angel, Delegacion Alvaro Obregón, Cd. Mexico.

One pair of pants had a handwritten note with a short message that is barely legible, *CIRUGÍA PLASTICA FACIAL, 14 DE ABRIL, 10* a.m. (Facial plastic surgery, April 14, 10 a.m.) Curiously, it is only fifteen days after April 14.)

A few hours later, the remains are wrapped in plastic tarps and tied with rope. They are transported to the Servicio Médico forense de la Ciudad de Mexico (Medical Forensic Service of Mexico City) for further examination and complete autopsies. Ventura then invites Villa into his office and they begin to develop a strategy for the investigation. Ventura and Villa are keenly aware that unless a drug connection is quickly found, the investigation will be given to the state police who have jurisdiction. They are also cognizant most murders in the country are linked to the drug trade and this one certainly has the classic brutal signature attached to it.

They decide to divide responsibilities; Ventura and his agents will conduct interviews of the families and hospital staff where it appears all three of the victims' work. They will also follow-up with the forensic examiners. Villa will coordinate with the DEA country office in Berlin regarding the chemical company and determine how their barrels ended up in Mexico. Both agree to communicate daily on their progress and findings. Villa knows that coordination and communication is key to any investigation, but even more so on bilateral cases with foreign counterparts.

Villa also plans on activating all of the agency's informants throughout Mexico in an effort to obtain more information on the bodies in the barrels. The DEA has an extensive global network of informants, which has been meticulously developed through time. The informants come from all walks of life, (*e.g.*, politicians, doctors, attorneys, prominent citizens, and criminals). Villa believes the best informants come from the criminal subculture. This is logical simply because of the comprehensive and insider information they are able to develop and provide on crime groups. He is well versed in the recruitment and handling of informants, which involves an understanding of their motivation to cooperate with the DEA. Some are motivated by fear of potential harm from associates or they wish to avoid a lengthy prison sentence. Others because of revenge, they feel slighted for a multitude of reasons. However, the vast majority of informants are mercenaries and they provide information for money. The motives can change through time and it is important to notice these changes. The skillful handling of sources of information is critical to ongoing investigations. Villa knows what psychological buttons to push with them such as cajoling, compliments, concern for them, allaying their fears, and many times subtle pressure. He is so experienced that he knows when they are lying or telling the truth. He has become a virtual human lie detector and never uses a polygraph to test their veracity.

In past years, Villa has seen the agency focus more and more on wire intercepts to the detriment of many other critical investigative tools. This leaves the agent workforce less skilled and prepared. He notices undercover work is becoming a dying art. Many of the younger agents have poor skills in conducting surveillances, tactical operations, interviews and interrogations, and the recruitment and handling of informants. He is deeply concerned because these are the fundamental "nuts and bolts" of the DEA tradecraft. Wires are important, but are only one tool of many that are also highly valuable.

The following day, Villa arrives at the office early in the morning and parks his car, a late model, dark blue Mercury Grand Marquis, in a secure parking lot behind the U.S. Embassy. Most vehicles used by Embassy personnel have diplomatic license plates, which stand out like a sore thumb. Villa has been able to get fictitious Mexican tags through local government contacts. It provides added security while traveling throughout Mexico. Moreover, the car can also be used while working undercover.

As he walks to the rear door, he can see a long line of Mexican citizens waiting to be interviewed by Consular officials for visas to travel to the United States. All of them have folders with documentation needed for their interviews. Villa knows many of them, despite waiting in line for hours, will be denied because they will be unable to prove financial solvency. This will be interpreted as increasing the possibility they will remain in the U.S. illegally to seek work. He sympathizes with them since they are only trying to escape extreme poverty and seek a better life. It also angers him because the drug traffickers using false documents with fat bank accounts are quickly given multiple entry visas.

Villa rapidly climbs the stairs and pulls out his embassy badge with his photo and flashes it to the young U.S. marine standing behind a thick bulletproof window. The marine pushes a button opening the lock on an even thicker steel door, which opens with a loud bang. Villa moves through the door and takes a nearby elevator to the fourth floor where the DEA offices are located. He sees his secretary, Ursula, who is from Sacramento down the hallway. Villa likes her; she is efficient and has exceptional interpersonal skills. Slight, her light brown hair and fair complexion, hints at a Spanish ancestry. What is important to Villa is that she speaks fluent

Spanish. This is absolutely critical to be effective in Mexico. Villa never understands why the agency continues to send personnel, including agents, who don't know a single word of the local language. They are unable to do their jobs since they can't communicate with local security forces, nor deal with informants, or even answer the telephones. It also increases the impact of "culture shock" and they withdraw to the confines of their offices and homes. This places a greater burden on those who do speak the language.

"Ursula, how are you this fine morning?"

"I am doing fine, Sir. I put this morning's teletypes and correspondence in your in-box."

"Thank you. Can you please get the DEA office in Berlin, Germany? I need to speak with Bob Mange, the Country Attaché."

"Certainly, I will dial the number now."

Minutes later, Ursula yells out, "I have Mr. Mange on the line for you. He's on extension 42."

"Bob, how the hell are you? I need your assistance on a joint investigation I'm conducting with the PGR (Mexican Attorney General's Office). We found human body parts in three barrels from a company named ChemCon in Stuttgart." Villa has Bob's undivided attention. The mention of dismembered bodies has that affect. Villa provides him with the serial numbers.

Bob replies, "I've been sick with bronchitis, but am on the mend. I have several German police contacts in Stuttgart and I will reach out to them immediately. They will get the information for me. You should come visit sometime and we can enjoy some great antipasto and pasta."

"I want to try some traditional German food like wiener schnitzel (breaded veal) or some wurst (sausage) when I go there. Besides, you know I could eat apfelstrudel (apple strudel) all day long," says Villa.

Bob chuckles. He is a tall Italian out of New York and a great agent. He has the appearance of a mafia don. He and Villa were previously assigned to the DEA Miami division and have become close friends. Bob is a fanatic about traditional Italian food and extremely loyal to his heritage and culture.

"Miguel, I will get back to you as soon as I get the information. Please keep in contact and let me know if you need anything else. Stay out of trouble."

"I will wait to hear from you and life would not be fun if I were not in trouble. It would also mean that I was not doing my job. Controversy follows those in the trenches, right? Call me when you have any information."

"Of course."

CHAPTER
3

THE INVESTIGATION

Villa works late into the night on paperwork he was unable to finish during the day. He is probably one of the few people still at the Embassy other than members of the marine security detail. One of them, a tall, clean shaven marine in a camouflage uniform comes through the DEA offices to check that all classified documents have been properly stored. He enters Villa's office and is surprised to see him.

He says, "Oh, excuse me, Sir. I didn't know you were still here... just doing a security sweep. Sorry for disturbing you."

"Not a problem. I will be here for another hour. Have a good night."

"You too, Sir."

Earlier in the day, Villa met with representatives from both the CIA and FBI to see if they had received any pertinent information from their human or technical sources (telephone or radio intercepts) regarding the bodies discovered in the barrels. Unfortunately, they haven't or are unwilling to share it, which is not uncommon. Villa is always perplexed about why intelligence and law enforcement agencies, all working for the security and stability of the same government, didn't engage in a mutually beneficial sharing of information. In his opinion, it only helped the criminals and terrorists who were able to operate in a more fluid and clandestine manner.

Leaving the Embassy, Villa is hungry and decides to grab a bite at his favorite "hole in the wall" restaurant, *El Caminero*, which specializes in tacos with tender chopped steak, grilled onions, and white cheese from the state of Chihuahua. They also make a great pico de gallo salsa that is regularly put on the tables in chipped, white soup bowls. The hearty well-seasoned, spicy garbanzo soup is also a favorite. Villa walks slowly to the establishment, which is less than two blocks from the Embassy.

The workers greet Villa when he walks in, "Senõr, cómo estás? Nos da gusto de verlo. Vas a lo de siempre con una Coca Cola light?" (Sir, how are you? We are happy to see you. Are you going to have the usual with a diet Coke?)

"Muy bien, gracias. Si lo mismo." (Very well, thank you. Yes, the same.)

The waiters all wear orange aprons and garrison style caps, which remind Villa of the Pilotka hats used by Russian pilots during World War II. Tacos are Villa's favorite food. However, the best in the world are from the *El Paragua* restaurant in his hometown. He always enjoys them when he returns home for a visit. He would often sit with Don Luis Atencio, the owner, for hours, during the evening, having a few shots of Don Julio tequila or a couple of glasses of red wine.

Villa is the only one in the unusually quiet little dive. He makes small talk with the waiters as they work over a large, sizzling grill. He remembers being there one day when a white stretch limousine pulled up in front and a bride and groom in full wedding regalia came in for some tacos. The bride's beautiful white wedding dress was full of grease by the time they left. She didn't appear to care. Villa wolfs down the delicious tacos he has covered with more salsa than the tortillas can hold and they fall apart in his hands.

When Villa finishes, he takes his orange plastic cup with multi-colored plastic chips to the cash register where they are counted and the bill is tallied with an old calculator. They resemble poker chips from a one-star casino and represent different menu items and drinks so when you place your order they put the corresponding chips in the cup that serves as your bill. When he steps outside, Villa stands for a few minutes in front of the Caminero observing the lonely street and the large moon that illuminates it. Behind him, the taco stand closes for the day and he hears the metal accordion type door being lowered with a rattling, clacking sound and the click of a padlock locking it to a ground anchor.

Villa walks along the uneven sidewalk back to the Embassy and is allowed entry after showing one of the security guards his credentials. As he pulls out of the parking lot, the guard lowers the large upright security metal barrier that prevents vehicles from ramming their way into the Embassy. On the way home, Villa thinks about the bodies that were found. He knows the killings were personal based on the savagery and use of torture, which served no purpose other than revenge in its most raw form. By leaving the barrels on the side of the road where they could be found, a message was obviously being sent to others. Undoubtedly, the killers are not people to be fucked with unless one had suicidal tendencies. He drives rapidly, bobbing and weaving in and out of traffic until he arrives at Bosques de las Lomas where he lives. After parking the car, he enters his house, a three-story fortress built literally on the side of a very steep mountain. The large windows provide a scenic view of the rolling green hills below and in the background stands a large Jewish synagogue illuminated by dozens of powerful security lights. Villa has been in the house during some of the largest and most powerful earthquakes that rocked Mexico City. On one occasion, he felt the house sway violently back and forth and was surprised that it didn't tumble down the mountain like a pile of wooden toothpicks. Still, earthquakes are the least of his worries.

Villa is exhausted, but he never sleeps more than three hours a night. He has conditioned himself to survive on little sleep and many times during operations will go three or more days without any rest. He sits on an oversized brown leather couch in his living room and watches a nauseating Mexican telenovela (soap opera), which he thinks are all terrible and poorly done. Unfortunately, they're the only television programs available in Mexico. They all deal with tragedies, conflict, misery, violence and dysfunctional fictional families.

Psychology students can easily use them as case studies in abnormal psychology.

In the early morning hours, Villa goes to bed and has a restless night. He is wondering where the investigation will take him and about the killers who are involved in the three horrific murders. After a couple hours, he wakes up and staggers to the shower praying that running water will be available today. Too frequently, it is not. He won't take any bets on the power either. The question is always: *will he have water or power today?* It is a game of chance that makes life interesting. He has candles stashed in each room and replaces them often, on these he can depend.

After leaving his house, Villa weaves through the early morning rush hour traffic and makes his way to work. Once at his office, he calls Larry Smith, the head of the National Security Agency (NSA) in Mexico.

"Larry, I need to talk to you about something I'm working on. Do you have a few minutes to come down to my office?"

"Sounds important. Sure, sure… I'll be down in a few."

Larry is a tall heavyset man with thick reddish hair who speaks with a distinguishable Texas twang. Villa appreciates his sense of humor and more so that he is not a fucking bureaucrat who embraces every bullshit rule or policy with religious fervor. Traditionally, the NSA provides information to the CIA and they, in turn, send a completely sanitized version to the DEA. It is watered down like English coffee and useless. Villa has established a close, personal relationship with Larry so he is able to get the information direct without having the CIA act as an intermediary.

The NSA is a great ally of the DEA and had assisted Villa six months earlier with the seizure of over four million dollars being sent through the Mexico City International Airport to Bogota, Colombia. The money was hidden in several large air conditioning units. Villa is one of the few individuals who understands NSA operations and uses the knowledge to his advantage. The NSA conducts global monitoring, collection, decoding, translating and analysis of information and data for foreign intelligence and counterintelligence purposes. This process is called *Signals Intelligence*. They monitor at least a billion people worldwide and hundreds of millions of telephones to obtain intelligence on terrorist activities and political/economic data deemed necessary for national security purposes.

Larry pokes his head through the doorway, "Hey, Miguel, where does the DEA hire its secretaries? Do you guys have active recruitment at all the beauty pageants?"
He laughs, "You know I'm being facetious."

"Larry, how are you? Thanks for coming," Villa greets him and laughs at his joke. "Listen, we found three dismembered bodies in 55 gallon barrels and the identifications in their wallets, which we are damn lucky to have recovered. The identifications reveal they are all prominent plastic surgeons. Have you collected any intelligence that might be related?"

Larry was pensive and responds, "We picked up something indicating that one of the major drug cartel leaders recently had plastic surgery and it didn't go well. We haven't figured out who he is, but apparently he was left disfigured... not a happy camper."

"Can you stay on those communications and let me know if you pick up anything more? I would really appreciate it."

"Of course, but it's going to cost you lunch."

"I will buy you the biggest steak in Mexico and add to your high cholesterol."

"You have a deal. Will keep you posted. See you soon."
"Thanks, Larry."

Villa then calls one of his best informants by the name of Rafael, best known as "La Serpiente" (The Snake). La Serpiente has a close relationship with many of the biggest drug trafficking networks in Mexico. He is dark skinned with very thick brown hair that always appears to be matted together. His face is pock marked from a bad case of acne when he was a teenager. He wears expensive clothes and lots of gold jewelry, but always looks like he has not bathed in weeks. Soap and water are incapable of making him look any better.

He was born in Culiacan, Sinaloa, and at any early age recruited and trained as a sicario (hitman) by local drug dealers. He made his first kill at the early age of thirteen. His target was a rival drug dealer who was in competition with his bosses. Rafael waited for him outside his house one evening and watched as he drove into the driveway. Nervously, Rafael quickly crossed the street with a Colt 45 in his right hand. The handle was too big for his small hand, but he was able to reach the trigger with his index finger. His victim stepped out his black SUV and saw Rafael point the gun at his chest. A blood-chilling scream pierced the night followed by three shots that reverberated in the clumped residential area. The trafficker fell heavily onto the concrete sidewalk after the bullets tore through flesh and bone, expanding as they tumbled through his body ripping internal organs to shreds. Rafael slowly walked up to him and pointed the barrel of his weapon at the dying drug dealer's head and fired one more round. He saw brain tissue mixed with dark red blood spill onto the ground. He felt bad for days, but any sense of morality evaporated as he continued to rack up more kills.

Years later, he served ten years in a miserable state prison for killing a municipal police officer. He became a highly respected sicario for being able to pull the trigger without hesitation. Villa knows that Rafael is a vicious career criminal, however, he is invaluable as a source of information regarding the biggest drug lords operating in the country. The best informants came from deep within the criminal underbelly. None of these men are likely to ever become priests.

"Rafael, cómo estas? Tres barriles con cuerpos desmembrados fueron encontrados en la carretera a Acapulco. Parece que los tres eran doctores en medicina. Necesito que hables con algunos de sus amigos y ver que saben acerca de esto." (Rafael, how are you? Three barrels with dismembered bodies were found on the road to Acapulco. It appears that all three were medical doctors. I need you to talk to some of your friends and see what they know about this.)

"Pobres diablos! Los que hicieron esto querian que sientan dolor antes de matarlos. Voy a hablar con algunos de mis compañeros y ver qué puedo averiguar." (Poor devils! Whoever did this wanted them to feel pain before killing them. I will talk to some of my associates and see what I can find out.)

"Por favor me llamas tan pronto que sabes algo." (Please call me as soon as you find out something.) Rafael responded,

"Por supuesto. Tengo un primo que sabe todo lo que está pasando. Lo llamaré enseguida. Cuídate." (Of course. I have a cousin who knows everything that is going on. I will call him right away. Take care of yourself.)

Later that afternoon, Villa receives a phone call from Bob Mange in Berlin. "Miguel, I have some information for you. We checked with ChemCon and the three barrels are part of a large shipment of ephedrine, a ton and a half to be precise, that was shipped to Mexico. It went by land through Spain and then by sea to the seaport of Veracruz, Mexico. The bill of lading shows it was paid in full, $97,500.00 in U.S. dollars, prior to being shipped. The purchaser is listed as Quimicas Mexico S.A. de C.V. located at Rio San Miguel #14, Fraccionamento Viveros del Rio, Toluca. Apparently, this company has purchased a total of twenty tons during the past five years based on ChemCon records."

Villa responds, "Bob, I really appreciate the information and I will be in touch. My regards to your family and hope to see you soon."

"Of course! Let me know if you need anything else."

Villa sits silently at his desk and mulls over the information. Ephedrine is an essential precursor for the manufacture of methamphetamine, a potent stimulant, which has created an epidemic of abuse in the U.S. Mexican organizations are purchasing ephedrine and pseudoephedrine in different countries such as Germany, India, and China. It is easily transformed into meth on a one to one ratio using a variety of conversion methods. In other words, a kilo of ephedrine will yield a kilo of meth or "speed" as it is called in street jargon. Traffickers were buying the ephedrine for $65.00 dollars a kilo and sold for $18,000 or higher on U.S. streets once it was converted to meth. The profit margin is phenomenal and it provides criminal organizations with hundreds of millions of dollars each year. Legitimately, ephedrine is used for cold and allergy remedies, but these huge quantities being sent to Mexico are big red flags. Hell yes, the amounts purchased by Quimicas Mexico are seriously suspicious for obvious reasons.

Villa places a telephone call to Comandante Ventura, which is quickly answered, but has a lot of static. "Florentino, can you hear me? I am getting static on the line."

"I am in an area that has poor cell coverage, but I can understand what you are saying. What is going on?"

"I received some interesting news from our Berlin office regarding the barrels. A ton and a half of ephedrine was shipped to Quimicas Mexico whose address is allegedly in Toluca. I am taking a drive in the morning to see if the address of the company is real."

"Miguel, I went to the hospital and interviewed the administrator. He said the three doctors are the top plastic surgeons in the country and highly regarded by their peers. He said they had literally dropped off the face of the earth and have been missing for days. My men also talked to the families who are worried because they have not heard from them for some time and fear the worst. They called the state police and reported the situation.

He laughed, "The state police couldn't find the Grand Canyon with a magnifying glass. One of the surgeons' wives told an interesting story. Her husband said he was approached about doing radical plastic facial surgery on a very wealthy and powerful man. He wanted the surgery to be performed at a private residence and was willing to pay double for the procedure. The doctor told his wife that he would have to remain with the patient for several days to help with his recovery. He was slightly unnerved by the circumstances and then never came home. This sounds entirely too coincidental and suspicious."

"It does sound very strange. Only a wanted criminal with a lot of money wants to completely change his appearance and it certainly sounds as though it is more extensive than just a cosmetic facelift. Can you also check with the Chamber of Commerce to see if Quimicas Mexico is a legitimate company?"

"Sure, I will do that in the morning and let me know how it goes in Toluca."

"We will be in touch. Call me on my cell if you need anything?"

Early the next day, Villa leaves his house and gets on the main highway to Toluca, which is thirty-nine miles west-southwest from Mexico City. He notices road crews are working hard on expanding and modernizing the highway. In the past, it was a very narrow two lane serpentine road and Villa had witnessed several unnecessary fatalities. Villa concludes that Mexican drivers think they are invincible. How else can one explain their stunningly erratic driving, if it is not a death wish? Two years earlier, a car had passed Villa on that same highway as though he were at a standstill. A few miles down the road the car had flipped on its roof and arms and legs were protruding from every window. The lunatic behind the wheel had wiped out an entire family.

Less than an hour later, Villa arrives in Toluca with its plush, green vegetation and encounters massive traffic jams that frustrate him more than anything else. Villa is not a laid back kind of guy and has always been very impatient with bumper-to-bumper traffic. He presses down on his horn as drivers ignore stop signs and traffic lights with blatant abandon as if this was some crazy in-vivo video game. Eventually, his blood pressure begins to drop as he enters the Portales downtown area and sees the beautiful gardens, parks, government buildings and museums. He passes by the Cosmovitral, a large building with large colorful, stained glass windows, which serves as a conservatory. His favorite landmark, however, is the cathedral with a looming dome supporting a bronze statue of Saint Joseph cradling the infant Jesus. It reminds him of the ornate mosques he visited in Istanbul, Turkey. On the outskirts of the city, he finally finds Rio San Miguel Avenue. He follows it and comes to an empty field filled with tall weeds and discarded garbage where Quimicas Mexico should be located. He has suspected as much, but had to verify his suspicions.

He quickly uses his cell to call Comandante Ventura, "Big surprise, Florentino, the fucking address is fictitious. It's an empty field with nothing on it except weeds and trash."

"Miguel, I also checked with a friend at commerce and Quimicas Mexico doesn't exist. Someone is merely using the name to import tons of ephedrine into Mexico, obviously to make methamphetamine."

"It certainly seems that way. Can you discretely check with the Customs people you totally trust at the port of Veracruz and see if they can tell us who picked up the ephedrine? You have to be extremely careful because some of them are undoubtedly involved. We also need to get copies of their paperwork."

"Ok, I will contact our agents in Veracruz and have them look into it."

"Thanks, Florentino. Let's get together soon and have dinner and a few tequilas."

"Sounds great as long as you are paying with your U.S. dollars. With all of the devaluations here, my pesos are almost worthless."

"Tell your politicians to quit stealing so much money and your peso would be worth ten times more than our dollars."

Both laugh and Florentino says, "It all started when the Spaniards conquered the Aztecs in 1521. Mexico didn't have any corruption until the Europeans came here. It has been worse than the smallpox virus they brought to our land." They chuckle since there is some truth to it.

Rain clouds move quickly into the area followed by a torrential downpour. Villa can barely see the highway so he decides to stop at the Loma Linda restaurant on the outskirts of Mexico City. He parks his car near the front entrance and sprints inside, but can't avoid getting soaked. He doesn't mind since he has always loved rain. As a small child he lived in a house with a tin roof and the pitter-patter of raindrops made him feel protected and his sleep much more pronounced. Villa is famished and orders grilled chicken and his favorite drink, fresh watermelon juice. Not long after, the waiter brings out a small Hibachi grill with the chicken, onions, and Serrano peppers still cooking over the hot charcoal. A round plastic tortilla warmer filled with freshly made corn tortillas comes with the meal. Villa is of the opinion, for some reason, the best chicken is found in Mexican restaurants.

As he is eating, Villa's phone rings and he barely hears it since it is deep in one of his pants pockets. It is Rafael calling from Culiacán, Sinaloa.

He says, "Hola, Miguel. Cómo estás? Tengo buenas noticias para usted. Ayer por la noche, me encontré con mi primo y me dijo que los médicos fueron contratados por José Atenco, el capo del Cártel Alianza de Sangre (Blood Alliance Cartel) para hacerle cirugía plástica en el rostro. Al parecer, durante la cirugía se produjo un corte de energía y en la obscuridad abrupto le dañaron algunos nervios, lo que le ha dejado con una desfiguración horrible. Su cara se parece a la cabeza de la muerte. Él se enfureció y ordenó a sus hombres para que torturar todos los médicos antes de matarlos." (Hi Miguel. How are you? I have some good news for you. Last night, I met with my cousin who said Jose Atenco, the boss of the Blood Alliance Cartel, had hired the three doctors to do plastic surgery on his face. Apparently during the surgery there was a power outage and in the abrupt darkness they damaged some nerves, which has left him with a horrible disfigurement. His face looks like a death's head. Enraged, he ordered his men to torture all of them before killing them.)

"Rafael, esta es una gran información. Su primo debe tener buenos contactos. Quién se lo dio?" (Rafael, this is great information. Your cousin must have great contacts. Who gave it to him?)

"Él es amigo de una de Atenco's amantes que vive en Culiacán. Ella dijo que Atenco se había convertido en un recluso ya que él no quiere que nadie vea su rostro. Según ella, él matará a cualquiera que se le queda mirando. Él ha dicho a sus hombres que nunca miren a la cara o él los quemara vivos. Él era un asesino antes de la cirugía, pero ahora es un asesino errática emocionalmente perturbado que golpeará con poca provocación." (He is a friend of one of Atenco's paramours who lives in Culiacán. She said that Atenco had become a recluse since he didn't want anyone to see his face. According to her, he will kill anyone who stares at him. He has told his men never to look at his face or he will have them burned alive. He was a killer prior to the surgery, but now he is an emotionally disturbed, erratic killer who will strike with little provocation.)

"Rafael, Su amante sabe dónde está? Como usted sabe es buscado por narcotráfico y asesinato en México y Estados Unidos." (Rafael, does his mistress know where he is? As you know he is wanted for drug trafficking and murder in Mexico and the United States.)

"Mi primo tiene miedo de preguntar muchas preguntas. Él tratará de obtener más información, pero muy lentamente. Él no es un hombre muy valiente. Él no quiere ni que la DEA sepa su nombre." (My cousin is afraid to ask many questions. He will try to get more information, but very slowly. He is not a very brave man. He doesn't even want the DEA to know his name.)

"Bien, tu necesitas mantenerte en cima de él para obtener más información. Anímelo a desarrollar una relación más estrecha con la amante. Esto es crucial, Rafael. Quedémonos en contacto." (Okay, you need to stay on top of him to get more information. Encourage him to develop a closer relationship with the mistress. This is crucial, Rafael. Let's stay in contact.)

"Horale, hablamos." (All right, we'll talk.)

After hanging up with Rafael, Villa calls Florentino and tells him of the significant information he has just received from Rafael on Atenco.

"We will have to proceed very carefully. Atenco is a ruthless psychopath who will kill based on nothing more than a whim. Life has absolutely no meaning for this man."

"Yes, I know and we have to put him behind bars where he belongs. I will see you tomorrow and we can discuss how we can get to him."

"Come early so we can have some sopa de Cahuama (Sea turtle soup).

CHAPTER 4

Alianza de Sangre Cartel

In the early morning, the loud squawk of a boisterous rooster brings to an end the deep sleep of the most feared and dangerous living thing in Mexico and quite possibly the entire western hemisphere. Jose Atenco, the undisputed head of the Blood Alliance Cartel, slowly opens his cold, reptilian looking green eyes. He shivers as the frigid mountain air sweeps silently through cracks in the windows of the large farmhouse hidden in the rugged mountains of Sinaloa.

It takes a few seconds for him to realize where he is since he changes locations every twenty-four hours. He is a wanted man and both the United States and Mexico each have a ten-million-dollar bounty on his head. Atenco is in a violent blood struggle with the Cartel del Norte (Cartel of the North) for control of the lucrative geographic areas along the U.S. border, which are used to smuggle tons of drugs to the insatiable U.S. consumer market.

He stares at the roof with the large round wooden beams and begins to reflect on the past few weeks. Atenco is deeply upset with himself and feels God has punished him for being so narcissistic and wanting to alter his face through plastic surgery. He hired the best surgeons in Mexico and still they managed to disfigure him. Now he is left with a permanently grotesque face. His entire face droops giving him the look of a gargoyle and his upper lip is so high, it exposes his gums and teeth leaving him with a menacing grimace. His rage was uncontrollable and he ordered his favorite assassin and associate, Humberto Flores, best known as *La Sombra* (The Shadow) to terrorize and torture the three surgeons. La Sombra doused their genitalia with water and then used a chicharra (cattle prod) to shock them with concentrated electricity. Atenco heard their screams as they pleaded for mercy and this only infuriated him even more. He felt that a man should die with dignity and not like old women begging for their lives.

Atenco yelled at them, "Hijos de putas, voy a matar a todos ustedes! Me jodiste y ahora tendran que pager con sus vidas miserables. Ustedes deben morir como hombres y no como los cobardes que son. Ustedes deben estar agradecidos de que no mato a todas sus familias!" (Sons of whores, I am going to kill all of you! You fucked me and now you will pay with your miserable lives. You should die like men and not like the cowards that you are. Be grateful that I don't kill your families!)

Atenco looked at La Sombra and said, "Quiero un mensaje enviado a todos que si chingan conmigo serán enviados al infierno en putos pedazos." (I want a message sent to everyone that if they fuck with me, I will send them to hell in fucking pieces.)

"Si jefe. Ellos pagarán por sus pecados en esta vida y la siguiente. No tienen honor y no son más que maricas. Por favor, deje sus minutos finales en este mundo en mis manos." (Yes, boss. They will pay for their sins in this life and the next. They have no honor and are nothing but fags. Please leave their final minutes on this earth in my hands.)

After being tortured for a couple of days, the surgeons, in abject horror, see La Sombra approach with a small chain saw.

"Por favor, señor, tener un poco de compasión. No hicimos nada intencional, fue un accidente y no es culpa nuestra. No tienes una pizca de decencia humana? Tenemos familias y niños pequeños." (Please Sir, have some compassion. We didn't do anything intentional; it was an accident and not our fault. Do you not have a shred of human decency? We have families and young children.) La Sombra chuckles loudly,

"Estoy a punto de practicar mis habilidades como carnicero y ustedes serán mis obras maestras." (I am about to practice my skills as a butcher and you will be my masterpieces.)

He pulls the cord of the chainsaw, which explodes into a deep roar. One at a time, La Sombra begins to slowly sever arms, legs, and heads as shrieks of terror and agony pierce the air. The dark red blood splatters in every direction and frayed chunks of flesh mixed with shards of bone begin to plaster the walls and ceiling. La Sombra, drenched in fresh, warm blood is always amazed at the primitive animalistic sexual pleasure he gets in killing. La Sombra takes the body parts and puts them in barrels and covers them with cement and the same day dumps them on the road to Acapulco. He makes sure the bodies will be found to send a clear message that you will die if you invoke the wrath of the Blood Alliance Cartel. La Sombra is well known throughout Mexico as the most feared and ruthless killer, but only a handful of people know what he actually looks like—most witnesses are dead. He always operates in the shadows, hence his name, and if the people he is going to kill happen to be blinking, they will die in darkness. He is ruthless and gruesomely lethal. The mere mention of his name grips even the most hardened criminals with fear and dread. It is rumored that he suffers from depression if more than a day passes without killing someone. He is the extreme version of a homicidal psychopath whose only passion is snuffing out lives.

Atenco is tall with an athletic build and his thick hair is beginning to gray. He had been a handsome man until the surgery left him painful to look at and even he has a hard time seeing his reflection in the mirror. Atenco grew up in the area of Culiacan, Sinaloa, in great poverty. His father, Abel, had a very small plot of land where he grew corn and sold it in the city. The money was not nearly enough to sustain a family of seven so Abel began to cultivate marijuana in the Sierra Madre Mountains. It was difficult work because of the rugged terrain and one had to literally live near the illicit crops to prevent others from stealing them. Abel would plant the marijuana seeds near the many mountain streams and use cheap, black rubber hoses to tap into the streams and irrigate the fields. Gravity carried the water to the strategically placed fields and he ensured that the plants had enough sunlight, which was required for the plants to survive and grow rapidly. Abel was able to usually get two harvests per year, and with luck maybe three.

Atenco hated his father because he was a drunk and became violent when he drank cheap moonshine made in the mountains. Most of his money was spent on alcohol and women and little for the family. Abel beat Atenco and all his brothers and sisters mercilessly. The mother, Maria, attempted to intercede, but it only angered Abel even more and he would batter her into unconsciousness.

Atenco, in order to help support his family, also began to grow marijuana and sold it at a hefty price to organized criminal groups operating in the area. They liked his marijuana because it was of high quality and well-manicured. He was able to ensure enough food was on the table every day and that his brothers and sisters had decent clothes. One day, he beat his father senseless after he caught him hitting his mother. He threw him out of the house and threatened to kill him if he ever returned. Fortunately, he never saw his father again.

Atenco, at an early age, saw the quick and enormous benefits of the drug trade and was in awe of the many drug lords that moved around the area in flashy trucks and were literally dripping in gold jewelry. They threw lavish parties and paid local bands to compose songs about their daring criminal exploits. Beautiful women were always dangling on their arms and they were spoiled with the best clothes and cars money could buy.

These were his only role models and he decided that his ultimate career goal was to become the greatest drug trafficker in the history of Mexico and maybe the world. He was driven and knew he was more cunning than most. He studied other traffickers and adopted their best methods and tactics. Atenco became extremely proficient in drug distribution, logistics, smuggling, concealment, money laundering, and corrupting public officials. He then took it to a higher level with strategic planning and created contingency plans to counter aggression by other drug dealers and government security forces.

Atenco also had a great dislike for corrupt government officials who ran the country and didn'thing to alleviate the massive poverty afflicting most of the population. They were not concerned with providing assistance programs or building schools to break the enslaving cycle of poverty. He saw politicians steal land from the poorest segment of society and line their pockets with millions of dollars. Atenco knew the only path to a better life was the drug trade and with the biggest consumer country nearby it is a rainbow with the proverbial pot of gold on the other side. He only has to have the guts to reach out and grab it.

Through time, Atenco begins to diversify his drug trafficking activities and enters the heroin trade. He cultivates large fields of amapola (opium poppies) near his marijuana fields. He hires poor young men from the area to help him during the harvesting of the opium gum. It is tedious work and labor intensive, but he pays them well. Days after the beautiful red petals fall from the pod, they use sharp razor blades imbedded in wooden handles to score the round pods. The blades are gauged so that the incisions are not too deep, which will cause the opium latex to leak into the center of the pod instead of the outside where it can be harvested. The pods have three ovarian walls and most of the opium is in the middle wall. The incisions are made horizontally at sunset because the hot sun will dry the latex quickly and prevent it from seeping out. The latex is initially white, but quickly oxidizes and turns brown. Atenco's workers then use curved knives to scrape the opium from the pods and place the wet gummy substance into gallon-size cans tied to their waists. The opium is initially converted into morphine base and then into heroin hydrochloride by chemists who have no education. They have learned the process while working as apprentices at clandestine laboratories near the poppy fields.

It takes ten kilograms of opium to make one kilo of heroin. Atenco's chemists produce black tar heroin since it is quick to make and has about a sixty-five percent purity level. Obviously, it isn't as refined and pure as Southeast Asian heroin, but it is highly popular. Each kilo sells in the U.S. for slightly over a hundred thousand dollars and is much easier to conceal and smuggle since it doesn't have the bulk of marijuana. The drug dealers in the U.S. mix the heroin with a wide variety of adulterants such as lactose, caffeine, glucose, and many other cutting agents for street sales. This allows them to make much more money, but it means taking more risk. Atenco doesn't care what they do since he has already made a huge profit on each kilo and his exposure is minimal.

By the time Atenco is in his mid-twenties, he is already a respected and feared drug trafficker by other much more established drug dealers. He has also amassed a great fortune, which he uses to build his mother and siblings a palatial mansion in the wealthiest section of Culiacan staffed by a small army of servants, gardeners, and security personnel.

He makes sure they don't want for anything. He is on his way to building a large, complex organization and more importantly a strong infrastructure to support it. As he expands his illegal business, Atenco hires the best aircraft pilots, boat handlers, chemists, ground transporters, money launderers, criminal attorneys and caretakers of the numerous stash sites located in the U.S. and Mexico. Very astutely, he also knows that his organization can't operate without the protection of government officials that he easily corrupts since he pays them more than they receive from their meager salaries. He allocates between ten and twenty percent of his profits to pay politicians and security forces to look the other way.

Atenco also likes playing the role of "Robin Hood" and builds churches and schools in various communities throughout Mexico. He gives money to homeless people living on the street or people who need help because of pressing medical problems. He is considered a great benefactor and the people protect him at all costs. If they observe any activity by the police or military in the area, they pass the information quickly to Atenco and his associates. It is a win, win situation for everyone.

Atenco has already carved out a coveted position in Mexico's underworld when he runs into La Sombra at a nightclub called Christine's in Puerto Vallarta. The music is blaring and the mirrored disco ball shoots rays of reflected light throughout the club. Atenco is sitting at a table surrounded by twenty fierce looking men who are armed to the teeth when he sees his old childhood friend enter the club dressed in traditional blue jeans, western shirt, and rattlesnake cowboy boots. La Sombra is a tall, muscular, handsome man who bears his trademark goatee. He walks with a swagger and his dark eyes dart back and forth constantly and take in everything around him. His face always has a menacing frown. He never smiles. He is a no nonsense man and humor is not something he understands or likes. Atenco and La Sombra's eyes lock on each other and they come together like magnets. La Sombra walks to Atenco and they immediately hug each other.

They attended grade school together and were both poor like all of the other students, but they have an air of confidence and didn't take any shit from any of the local bullies. They played together, shared food, and whatever little possessions they were able to obtain. Both are extremely tough and highly intelligent. At an early age, they showed a natural instinct for leadership and other kids followed them without hesitation.

Atenco and La Sombra protected them from those that bullied them and took their money. Both friends show their cunning and willingness to handle problems with extreme violence. One of the smaller students was roughed up after school by three older kids who stole the few cents he had in his pocket. The following day, Atenco and La Sombra spread the word that one of the students had quite a bit of money. They watched as the three thugs ran up to him as he walked home from school. Atenco and La Sombra were ready and they jumped out of the bushes and beat the three boys senseless with baseball bats. The cracking sound of the bats and loud screams were heard for half a mile. Bloodied and unconscious, the thugs were left in the dirt and understandably never bothered anyone again.

La Sombra never knew the father who abandoned him two months after he was born. His mother, Anita, laundered other people's clothes and sold tortillas she made in order to survive. The house they lived in had a dirt floor and an outdoor toilet. Most of the windows were shattered and the doors were so rotted they provided little protection against the elements. La Sombra adores his mother and she is the only soft spot in his heart. He later became a hired assassin for several drug traffickers when he was just fourteen years old. A petty criminal made the mistake of kidnapping the daughter of a local drug dealer and asked for a fifty-thousand-dollar ransom. It was paid and the girl was released. Several weeks later, a close associate gave the drug dealer the name of the kidnapper. That sealed his fate. La Sombra was contracted to kill him for only a hundred dollars. He was given a black revolver with rubber bands wrapped around the handle so it could be hidden in the waistband and the rubber bands, through friction, would hold it in place. It took a week for La Sombra to find the man who was staying with a cousin in a nearby village. One hot morning, he saw the kidnapper leave the house and walk down the dusty dirt road towards a nearby cantina. When he was about six feet away,

La Sombra yells out to him, "Oye, hijo de puta. Soy La Sombra y estoy aquí para enviarle a conocer a tu creador antes de lo que usted gustaría." (Hey, you son of a whore. I am The Shadow and I am here to send you to meet your maker sooner than you would like.)

The man turned quickly and when he saw La Sombra, he began to howl in laughter. The humor only lasted a few seconds and quickly changed when La Sombra jerked the weapon out from his tattered pants and pointed it at his human target. The first shot hit the kidnapper in the center of his chest, which he clutched with both hands as he let out a loud gasp. He grimaced with pain and the last thing he heard was one final boom, a split second before the hot piece of lead tore into his right eye and penetrated his gray matter. His heart stopped pumping before he hit the ground. It was the only time La Sombra felt a tinge of remorse. By the time he was eighteen, he had murdered over thirty men, mostly other criminals. And, with time, he perfected his craft and became the perfect hunter. He was cold, calculating, patient, and very cunning. All of these are good attributes for an efficient executioner.

Eventually, the men who hired him become fearful of La Sombra. They knew one day, he would go after them and they would die like all the ones who now populated dozens of cemeteries filled by La Sombra. They put out a fifty thousand dollar contract on La Sombra, but he found out from another assassin who had befriended him and told him of the plans to end his life. Before fleeing from the area, La Sombra, one night, paid visits to three expensive houses and killed the men for their treachery. He butchered them with a long, serrated, double-edged dagger. Then he executed their wives for good measure. The red blood dripped off the beds onto the carpet in a small stream. Before leaving, he used some white bed sheets and left messages with blood the blood of his victim's. They read:

MUERTE A TODOS LOS QUE CHINGAN CON LA SOMBRA. (DEATH TO ALL WHO FUCK WITH LA SOMBRA.)

He hung the sheets on the wall and left as quietly as he had entered.

Atenco, despite the blaring music at Christine's, greets his old friend. "Mi viejo amigo, es el destino que una vez más nos une. Ha pasado mucho tiempo desde que nuestros caminos se han cruzado. Dónde diablos has estado?" (My old friend, it is destiny that once again unites us. It's been a long time since our paths have crossed. Where the hell have you been?)

"José, tienes razón que ha pasado mucho tiempo desde que te he visto. La vida, como usted bien sabe, tiene muchas sorpresas algunas buenas y otras malas. He tenido la suerte de sobrevivir incluso las malas situaciones. Es bueno verte, amigo mío." (Jose, you're right it's been a long time since I've seen you. Life, as you know, has many surprises, some good and some bad. I've been lucky enough to survive even the bad situations. Good to see you, my friend.)

"Por favor, tome asiento y bebe un poco de tequila conmigo. Yo no te puedo decir lo contento que estoy de verte después de tantos años. Había oído que usted estaba haciendo trabajos para muchas personas en nuestro tipo de negocio. Me alegro de que la Virgen María ha sonreído en usted y lo ha protegido." (Please, take a seat and drink some tequila with me. I cannot tell you how happy I am to see you after all these years. I heard that you were doing work for many people in our type of business. I am glad that the Virgin Mary has smiled on you and protected you.)

The mood is festive and the tequila flows like water. Both Atenco and La Sombra relax as they remember their early childhood years. Despite the staggering hardships, they have good memories growing up in the Sierra Madre Mountains, which provided them with many adventures playing the role of famous bandits who gained fame in the area by stealing from the rich and giving to the poor. They use small tree branches and pretend they're rifles and chase each other in the plush, green vegetation along the mountain streams. On occasion, they'd steal corn, melons, and cabbages, which they took home to their families. Initially, their poverty is masked by their innocence, but as they grow older, it is lifted and they become aware that unless they are willing to take risks life will quickly end without having enjoyed even a few pleasures in life. They decide it is better to live one good year than ten bad ones and thus the die is cast. Both have made their fortunes in the drug trade, but it is not easy money as most people think. They live in a world filled with treachery and violence. The government relentlessly pursues them and rival cartels want to kill them. They are hunted men who trust no one and understand that today's friend could be to-morrow's enemy.

The music blasts and the loud animated chatter from the patrons makes it difficult to hear anything else. Suddenly, screams can be heard above the din of hard rock music as four men enter the discotheque brandishing Ak-47s. The gunmen's eyes have not yet adjusted to the dark interior and they begin to randomly spray the club with explosive bursts of high velocity rounds hoping to hit Atenco, their intended target. Chaos, within seconds, is rampant as the automatic weapons spew fire and lead splinters wood furniture, and shards of glass fly through the air. Bodies raked with bullets move in a grotesque dance of death as blood sprays the walls and floors. The screams intensify as people dive to the floor into large, expanding pools of sticky, dark red blood.

With blinding speed, La Sombra, pulls his black, lethal Beretta .9mm out of his waistband and fires four shots in a rapid blur. All four assassins fall lifeless to the floor next to each other. La Sombra struts, nonchalantly over to where the four dead gunmen are sprawled. All of them have bullet holes between their eyes. His aim is flawless. He honed his craft as a professional sicario carrying out nearly impossible missions. Bloody brain matter oozes from the exit wounds in the back of their heads. The screeches of fear and the groans of the dying and wounded don't faze La Sombra as he is devoid of compassion and empathy. He returns to Atenco who is now surrounded by his security escorts who have their weapons out and are pointing them in every direc-tion.

La Sombra calmly says, "José, sé quien son estos cabrones. Son sicarios profesionales que son miembros de Los Rojos que trabajan para Albino Romero, jefe del Cartel del Norte. Él va a seguir tratando de matarte. Es necesario llegar a él primero." (Jose, I know these motherfuckers. They are professional killers, members of Los Rojos that work for Albino Romero, head of the Cartel of the North. He'll continue trying to kill you. You need to get to him first.) Atenco very pensively responds,

"Tarde o temprano, voy a poner mis manos en ese hijo de puta y él arrepentiré conocerme. Voy a despellejar al bastardo con mis propias manos y alimentar a mis perros con su cuerpo. Vamonos antes de que llegue la policía. Agarran las armas de estos idiotas y vamos a usarlas contra el Cartel del Norte." (Sooner or later, I'll get my hands on that son of a whore and he will repent knowing me. I will skin the bastard with my own hands and feed his body to my dogs. Let's go before the police arrive. Grab the idiot's weapons and we will use them against the Cartel of the North.) La Sombra, Atenco, and the large security escort pile into six black armored Chevy Suburbans and the sound of numerous doors slamming shut fill the night air. With tires squealing, they speed off into the darkness.

The assassination attempt now brings Atenco and La Sombra together in an unholy alliance that will bring untold savagery and wholesale violence to Mexico. More than all of its military wars combined.

CHAPTER
5

Blood Feud

I t is a hot day in the dusty, isolated mountainous region of Badiraquato, Sinaloa. Some of the world's most ruthless drug traffickers sit around a massive oak table full of all kinds of fruits and a vast assortment of meats and sausages heaped on large platters. At the center of the table are at least a dozen bottles of the best tequila money can buy. Four bowls with slices of fresh lime are at each corner of the table. The twelve men, in faded blue jeans and expensive boots, look rugged and have cruel, menacing stares. They are the regional bosses of the Blood Alliance Cartel and all have proven their worth by spilling the blood of politicians, reporters, police, judges, and any person who stands in the way of their violent business. Once they are all settled in, Atenco enters the room with an air of supreme self-confidence and addresses the upper hierarchy of his vast criminal empire. "He llamado a todos ustedes aquí porque tenemos un grave problema que tenemos que enfrentar de inmediato. Como ustedes bien saben, los putos perros del Cartel del Norte están tratando de apoderarse de nuestro territorio y han matado a muchos de nuestros hombres. Estoy dando la orden de matar a todos ellos. Voy a utilizar nuestros buenos amigos de la pandilla Barrio Maya en El Paso, Texas para cazarlos a mil dólares por cabeza. Quiero usar a ellos, ya que pueden volver a los EE.UU. en cualquier momento que tienen que huir de las autoridades de aquí." (I have called you all here because we have a serious problem we have to confront immediately. As you know, the fucking dogs from the Cartel of the North are trying to take over our territory and have killed many of our men. I'm giving the order to kill them all. I will use our good friends from the Barrio Maya gang in El Paso, Texas to hunt and kill them for a thousand dollars a head. I want to use them because they can return to the US any time they have to flee from the authorities here.)

One of his men responds, "Todos apoyamos su plan de aniquilar a los bastardos del Cartel del Norte. Tenemos que enviar un mensaje de que no sólo vamos a matarlos, pero vamos a decapitar y desmembrar a ellos. Esta es la única cosa que respetarán. El miedo es la clave de nuestro negocio. No usar trajes y caminar alrededor de las oficinas como tantos burócratas. Somos hombres con las bolas que no tienen miedo de matar o morir. Nuestro cartel tiene que ser el más malo y más violenta de México con el fin de intimidar aquellos que quieren hacernos daño. Esto debe incluir esos hijos de puta que se hacen llamar periodistas. Siempre nos identifican por nombre y con fotos en sus periódicos de mierda. Todos estamos juntos en esto de los nuestros." (We all support your plan to annihilate the bastards from the Cartel of the North. We must send a message that we will not only kill, but we will decapitate and dismember them. This is the only thing they respect. Fear is the key to our business. We don't wear suits and walk around the office like so many bureaucrats. We are men with balls that are not afraid to kill or be killed. Our cartel has to be the meanest, most vicious in Mexico in order to intimidate those who want to do us harm. This should include those bastards who call themselves journalists. They are always identifying us by name and in photos in their shit newspapers. We are all in this thing of ours together.)

Atenco continues, "Quiero establecer un pequeño almacén en las afueras del sur de la ciudad de Juárez, donde podemos almacenar armas y municiones que serán utilizados por la pandilla Barrio Maya cuando cruzan a matar a los perros desde el Cartel del Norte. Quiero pistolas, rifles de asalto AK-47, granadas y granadas propulsadas por cohetes disponibles. También me gusta la estrategia utilizada por ISIS y vamos a adoptar el mismo modelo de terror y violencia. Esto también hará que la policía federal y el ejército nos temen también. Además, todos ustedes son para recoger información sobre dónde viven nuestros enemigos; qué tipo de coches que conducen; donde se congregan; ubicación de almacenamiento de drogas áreas, nombres de funcionarios y periodistas que están en sus bolsillos." (I want to set up a small warehouse in the southern outskirts of the city of Juarez, where we can store weapons and ammunition to be used by the gang Barrio Maya when they cross to kill the dogs from the Cartel of the North. I want pistols, AK-47 assault rifles, hand grenades, and rocket-propelled grenades available. I also like the strategy used by ISIS and we will adopt the same model of terror and violence. This will also make the federal police and army fear us. In addition, all of you are to collect information on our enemies, where they live; what kind of cars they drive; where they hang out; locations of drug storage areas; names of officials and journalists who are in their pockets.)

"Jefe, todos estamos de acuerdo con usted y llevará a cabo sus órdenes. Usted tendrá que utilizar sus conexiones políticas con el fin de desviar sus acciones lejos de nosotros y llevar a sus recursos contra el Cartel del Norte. Con la ayuda de la policía federal y militar podemos terminar estos bastardos. Nosotros no tenemos que preocuparnos por la policía estatal y municipal, puesto que ya están en nuestros bolsillos." (Boss, we agree with you and will carry out your orders. You will have to use your political connections in order to divert their actions away from us and bring their resources against the Cartel of the North. With the help of the federal and military police, we can end these bastards. We don't have to worry about the state and municipal police, since they are already in our pockets.)

"Bien, pero recuerda, tenemos que mantener nuestro negocio funcionando sin interrupción. Esta guerra nos va a costar mucho dinero y vamos a tener que aumentar nuestros pagos a nuestros amigos políticos. Entendido?" (Okay, but remember, we have to keep our business running without interruption. This war is going to cost a lot of money and we have to increase our payments to our political friends. Understood?)

That evening, after drinking numerous two thousand dollar bottles of Jose Cuervo, 1800 Coleccion, aged in French oaked barrels, Atenco and his men are in a festive mood. In their culture, business always has to be mixed with pleasure. Some of the best looking prostitutes from the area are brought to the isolated ranch house to participate in the revelry. One of the most popular ranchero musical bands, Los Grandes del Sur, is transported in with their musical instruments sticking out from the windows of several dark sedans. The first song, a narco corrido (drug ballad), which they composed to honor Atenco starts with the deep sound of the trombone, followed by the guitar, trumpets and the polka beat of the accordion. The male singer, dressed in a bright red outfit with frill around the shoulders and arms, sings loudly into the microphone.

"Soy José Atenco y nadie se atreve a meterse conmigo; nacido en la tierra de los aztecas, soy un verdadero guerrero;

Mis armas están hechas de acero, el Ak-47 y Colt .45;

Temido por todos los hombres y amado por las mujeres;

Yo soy un héroe para los pobres y desafortunados;

El gobierno trata de matarme;

Pero soy astuto y escurridizo como las sombras;

Un día, voy a morir, pero va a estar en mis pies como un hombre:

Soy José Atenco, jefe del Cartel Alianza de Sangre. He venido de la pobreza y la miseria;

El gobierno nunca ayudó a su gente y sólo a sí mismos llenarse los bolsillos con dinero de la sangre y sudor de su gente;

Sin oportunidades abrimos la única puerta a nuestra disposición, el tráfico de droga era nuestra única salvación y nosotros lo abrazamos;

Nuestro negocio no es para aquellos que carecen de las bolas y tienen miedo a morir;

Soy José Atenco, jefe del Cartel Alianza de Sangre.

Los malditos gringos robaron nuestra tierra y ahora se quejan de mi pueblo y se refieren a ellos como inmigrantes no deseados;

Con mi polvo blanco, ahora robo sus almas miserables; siembro violencia en sus ciudades y yo soy su ángel de la muerte que tomará sus vidas por miles;

Voy a joder a ellos y su país hipócrita;

Soy José Atenco, jefe del Cartel Alianza de Sangre."

(I am Jose Atenco and no one dares to mess with me; born in the land of the Aztecs; I am a true warrior;

My weapons are made of steel, the Ak-47and Colt .45; feared by all men and loved by women; I'm a hero to the poor and unfortunate; the government tries to kill me; but I am cunning and elusive as the shadows; one day I will die, but It will be on my feet like a man;

I am Jose Atenco, head of the Blood Alliance Cartel. I came from poverty and misery;

The government never helped those in need and only filled their pockets with money from the blood and sweat of its people;

Without opportunities we opened the only door available to us; drug trafficking was our only salvation and we embraced it;

Our business is not for those without balls and afraid to die;

I am Jose Atenco, head of the Blood Alliance Cartel;

The fucking gringos stole our land and now they complain about my people and refer to them as unwanted immigrants;

With my white powder, now I steal their miserable souls; sow violence in their cities; and I am the angel of death who will take their lives by the thousands;

Fuck them and their hypocritical country; I am Jose Atenco, head of the Blood Alliance Cartel.)

Later that night as the party is beginning to wind down, one of Atenco's men takes the microphone and says, "Jefe, tenemos un regalo especial para ti. Usted ha hecho todos nosotros hombres ricos y poderosos y estamos muy agradecidos. Ahora tenemos control sobre el cincuenta por ciento del tráfico de drogas en los Estados Unidos y hemos ampliado nuestro negocio para incluir también la metanfetamina. Nuestros ingresos el año pasado fue más de quince mil millones de dólares y este año será aún más. Nos hemos expandido a más de setenta países y están en el proceso de establecer más redes en Europa y el Medio Oriente. Por favor acepte esta botella muy especial de tequila. Es Ley 0.925 Tequila Pasion Azteca Ultra Premium Añejo, la edición Diamond Sterling, la botella es la más cara tequila en el mundo. Gracias por todo. Salud!" (Boss, we have a special gift for you. You have made all of us rich and powerful men and we are very grateful. Now we have control of over fifty percent of the drug trade in the United States and we have expanded our business to include methamphetamine. Our revenue last year was more than fifteen billion dollars and this year we will make even more money. We have expanded to more than seventy countries and are in the process of establishing more networks in Europe and the Middle East. Please accept this very special bottle of tequila. It is Ley 0.925 Pasion Azteca Ultra Premium Tequila Añejo, the Diamond Sterling Edition, the most expensive bottle of tequila in the world. Thanks for everything. Cheers.)

The bottle is made of pure platinum and encrusted in diamonds. It is worth three and a half million dollars, but to members of the Blood Alliance Cartel it is like buying a cheap bottle of tequila to anyone else.

Early in the morning, everyone wakes up at the crack of dawn with a throbbing hangover that makes even the sound of a closing door seem like an atomic explosion. The prostitutes had left at least an hour earlier since they had another engagement in a nearby town. Time is money and they chase after it like the flag chasers in Dante's Inferno. After a hearty breakfast of eggs, chilaquiles, Qaxacan chorizo, and warm tortillas, the pain seems to go away. After giving each other the traditional Mexican abrazo (hug), the drug traffickers and their heavily armed security escorts pile into their vehicles and drive off in clouds of dust. Atenco and La Sombra watch from the porch as they leave as quickly as they had come.

Atenco stands quietly for a few minutes and then looks at La Sombra. "Ahora empezamos una guerra de desgaste, pero que nos dará el control total del tráfico de drogas en México. La Sombra, como mi buen amigo que siempre he confiado, te estoy haciendo el segundo al mando del cártel. Te enseñaré todo lo que tienes que saber. Va a ser perfecto, ya que teme a nadie y confía en nadie." (Now we start a war of attrition, but it will give us total control of drug trafficking in Mexico. La Sombra, as my good friend whom I have always trusted, I'm making you the second in command of the cartel. I'll teach you everything you need to know. You will be perfect as you fear no one and trust no one.)

"Gracias, José. No te decepcionaré. Juntos, vamos a hacer el cartel aún más fuerte e indestructible." (Thanks Jose. I will not let you down. Together, we will make the cartel even stronger and indestructible.)

Less than two weeks later, a well-placed informant within the Cartel of the North calls La Sombra and tells him several members of the cartel were getting together for a party in Hidalgo de Parral, Chihuahua. He says the party will be held the following Tuesday at 8:00 p.m. and it is to celebrate the birthday of one of the important cartel regional bosses who lives in the city. He describes the house as an expensive single story, colonial style home painted light brown with a subtle red trim. The informant says the house is located on Carretera Santa Barbara, kilometro 5.6, and is close to the Rio Parral.

La Sombra immediately advises Atenco and they made plans for the attack. An hour later, La Sombra goes to a pay phone and calls David Velarde, head of the Barrio Maya gang. Velarde is tall, lanky, and his light brown hair is always combed to the side, but always appears disheveled. He is also a made member of the Mexican Mafia and has a black hand with an M in the middle tattooed on his left chest. The violent gang, while Velarde was serving a ten-year prison sentence in San Quentin for murder, recruited him. One day, he was given the "green light" to kill a couple of inmates who ripped off the Mexican Mafia for a few ounces of heroin. He prepared a shank made from a piece of metal from the prison workshop, which he sharpened at night in his cell against the metal bunk. In order to avoid cutting himself, he wrapped one of his socks around it as a makeshift handle. Two days later, he walked into the laundry area and savagely stabbed one of the inmates in the carotid artery and quickly pulled it out and drove the blade into the chest of the second inmate in rapid succession. The inmates nearby walked away and Velarde knew they would keep their mouths shut. To do otherwise was a death sentence in prison. The dying inmates gasped for air as they went into shock from the loss of blood. Less than ten minutes later, they stopped moving and were completely soaked in their own blood. Velarde had ten tear-drops tattooed down his cheeks from each of his eyes. Each one stood for a murder he had committed as a gang member.

After being released from prison, he returned to El Paso, his birthplace and created the feared Barrio Maya gang. Within a few years they began to make millions of dollars providing security, doing assassinations, and distributing drugs for the Blood Alliance Cartel. They are careful to speak in code in the event the calls were being intercepted.

La Sombra says, "David, vamos a tener una barbacoa donde Pancho Villa cerró los ojos por el ultimo tiempo. Tienes que ir al almacén y recoger algunos equipos. Necesitamos unas diez personas para que podamos pasar un buen rato. Usted necesita reunirse conmigo en la principal ciudad del sur de ustedes y desde allí puedemos ir a la fiesta juntos." (David, we are going to have a barbecue where Pancho Villa closed his eyes for the final time. You have to go to the warehouse and pick up some equipment. We need about ten people so we can have a good time. You need to meet me in the main city south of where you are at and from there we can go to the party together.)

Barbecue is code that someone is going to be murdered and Hidalgo de Parral is where Villa had been assassinated in 1923 and it was there that he had closed his eyes permanently. David also knows that the main city is Chihuahua, Chihuahua, which is the capital city and that equipment stood for weapons.

"Entendido. Voy a empezar a hacer arreglos de inmediato. Cuándo quieres encontrar en la ciudad principal?" (I understand. I'll start making arrangements immediately. When would you like to meet at the main city?)

"Este próximo domingo. Yo estaré allí temprano en la mañana y luego podemos dejar ese mismo día a la barbacoa donde se llevará a cabo. Todo tiene que estar listo en la madrugada del martes." (This coming Sunday. I'll be there early in the morning and then we can leave that same day to where the barbecue will be held. Everything has to be ready by early Tuesday morning.)

Velarde replies, "Entiendo cada pinche cosa que necesitamos para estar listo para deshacerse de estos rabiosos perros. Nos vemos el domingo." (I understand every fucking thing that we need to do to get rid of these rabid dogs. See you on Sunday.)

Early Sunday morning, La Sombra takes AeroMexico flight 234 nonstop to Chihuahua, Chihuahua. The plane is almost empty and he is happy that he didn't have to listen to screaming kids or deal with someone wanting to make small talk. He mulls over the operational plan that has been carefully developed that will snuff out the lives of several ranking members of the Cartel of the North. La Sombra is a strategist and doesn't like to leave anything to chance in carrying out his deadly missions. He covers every potential contingency in his mind over and over again and makes adjustments until he is completely satisfied.

He has the flight attendant serve him a double shot of tequila so he can get some sleep. The tequila is a cheap brand and tastes like diesel fuel, but it does the trick. La Sombra nods off into a deep sleep and dreams about his favorite

thing, violence. He smiles broadly as vivid thoughts of murder enter his dreams. A couple of hours later, La Sombra
awakes to the voice of the pilot loudly declaring that they
were starting their downward descent into Chihuahua, Chihuahua. He quickly makes a trip to the restroom and splashes
cold water on his face to refresh himself. Once the plane
lands and taxies slowly to the gate, La Sombra grabs his
carry-on bag containing two changes of clothes. He doesn't
plan on being in Chihuahua for very long. As he exits the
airport, he spots a brown Toyota Land Cruiser approaching
and recognizes Velarde and a few of his men.

Velarde jumps out of the car and hugs La Sombra, "Como
fue el viaje? Llegamos tarde la noche anterior y me traje diez
de mis mejores hombres. Estamos alojados en dos hoteles
separados por lo que no llamara demasiado la atención.
Tenemos armas suficientes para tomar control de todo el estado de Chihuahua." (How was the trip? We arrived late last
night and I brought ten of my best men. We are staying in
two separate hotels in order not to attract too much attention.
We have enough weapons to take over the entire state of Chihuahua.)

La Sombra responds, "Perfecto! Vamos al hotel donde me
alojo y podemos hablar de lo que hay que hacer. Por cierto,
Atenco envía sus saludos." (Perfect! Let's go to the hotel
where I am staying and we can talk about what we need to
do. By the way, Atenco sends his greetings.)

La Sombra is quiet as they drive into the city of Chihuahua. He notices that the poor keep getting pushed away from
the richer central part of the city by a powerful centrifugal
force created by corrupt politicians. Their homes are poorly
constructed and time has rapidly decayed them to the point
of collapse. They have large, cheap metal advertising signs

nailed to the outer walls, which provide the only color to the drab adobe structures. Continuing on into the heart of the city, La Sombra sees the beautiful Spanish Baroque Cathedral on the Plaza de Armas that is in the shape of a Latin cross. He looks at the Palacio de Gobierno (Palace of Government), which is an expensive, ornate neoclassical building and wonders why the government needs such an ostentatious building when so many people live in cardboard shanties. It angers him. The Museo de la Revolucion (Museum of the Revolution) catches his eye as they drive slowly past it. He knows it had been the former home of the legendary Pancho Villa. La Sombra would have liked to have stopped and seen the bullet riddled 1919 Dodge Roadster that Villa and two of his bodyguards were driving when they were ambushed and killed in Hidalgo de Parral in 1923. La Sombra thinks to himself that they are about to, once again, bring murder to the doorstep of the city. It is in our DNA, he thought.

On arrival at the hotel, Velarde calls all his men and has them come to his room one at a time so as not to arouse the suspicions of other guests or the hotel management. Once they are all there, he calls La Sombra who enters the room and everyone immediately understands that he is a force to be reckoned with and he sends chills into the very souls of the hardened criminals.

Within two hours, La Sombra has laid his plan and the roles of each individual. He doesn't want anyone to escape the deadly trap that will result in great human carnage. The more savage the better. It will put uncontrollable fear into the hearts and minds of those who are part of the Cartel of the North and the corrupt officials who protect it. He instructs two of the gang members to drive by the target residence and reconnoiter the area to identify places that can be used to conceal the attack team. La Sombra wants to have everyone in place by early Tuesday morning. After he gets the information on the house and surrounding area, he will make final changes to the plan.

Two hours later, the gang members return and draw a rustic, but detailed map of the house and surrounding area. The house is somewhat isolated and close to a sparsely traveled road. Directly across the road is a large field of tall weeds. Behind the house are rolling hills covered by heavy brush and tall pine trees.

One of the security features of the house is the wrought iron on all the windows and doors. La Sombra also assumes they will have armed guards posted on the front door. He also surmises that the other doors will also be guarded. La Sombra is a deliberate and cautious man.

La Sombra gives his final briefing regarding the attack on the Cartel of the North. He will post two snipers each at the front and back of the house armed with M2010 enhanced sniper rifles equipped with AN/PVS-29 clip-on sniper night sight scopes and silencers. The weapons weigh five and a half kilograms and use Winchester Magnum ammunition in detachable magazines that have a five round capacity. They are extremely deadly since they have an effective range of one thousand three hundred yards.

The snipers will be responsible for initially taking out the security guards outside the house and then anyone who survives the initial onslaught and tries to escape. He also posts two other men, one at the front and the second one in the rear of the house who are armed with Soviet made RPG-7s, which are anti-tank grenade launchers to blast through the doors and walls of the house.

The grenade launchers weigh seven kilograms and each grenade about two kilos. The weapon has an effective range of two hundred yards and is equipped with 1PN 58 Night Vision sights. Once launched, the grenades have a velocity of two hundred and ninety-five meters per second. The sniper and RPG teams will be at a safe distance in order to avoid killing each other in crossfire. A third group with fully automatic AK-47s will then assault the house and finish off any survivors. La Sombra will set up half a mile from the area. It is closer to the city and he will provide a rear guard in the event of a response by local police. He will have a .50 caliber Browning submachine gun AN/M2 with armor piercing-incendiary-tracer rounds. The devastating bullets are distinguishable by its red tips with an aluminum colored ring. It is belt-fed and capable of firing lead projectiles at a rate of one thousand two hundred per minute. It is definitely the ultimate killing machine. It weighs slightly less than sixty kilos. La Sombra will need two men to carry it to the site where it will be positioned.

The Blood Alliance Cartel doesn't have any problems getting weapons, with the vast majority coming from the US. Drugs flowed north and weapons moved south. They pass each other at the border. Most of the weapons were bought at gun shows and private sales. Some were stolen from military stockpiles and then smuggled into Mexico. Military grade weapons were also hugely available from the wars in Central America that had been furnished by the US. The cartel also took advantage of the fact that one eighth of the Mexican army deserts every year and the deserters take their government issued automatic weapons with them when they leave. The deserters sold them for needed cash.

La Sombra provides each member of the team with a Motorola VHF/UHF two-way radio to make sure everything is properly coordinated. La Sombra tells the gang members that after the ambush they will travel south to the city of Gomez Palacio, Durango. All the weapons will be put in false compartments of a tractor-trailer and transported back to the warehouse in Juarez. From there they will go an additional fourteen miles to Torreon, Coahuila and then take a direct commercial flight to Juarez. La Sombra, however, will take a flight to Culiacan, Sinaloa. He makes plans to have everyone in place during the early morning hours of Tuesday under the cover of darkness. The assault team on the house will have to walk several miles in a circuitous route to avoid detection. They will carry enough food and water to sustain them for an entire day.

The members of the assassination team go to bed early. Carrying out mass killings is hard and complex work and requires a clear mind and mental focus otherwise the hunters could end up being the prey. It is easy to kill civilians because they are naïve and careless. It is a different story when you went after other criminals who don't trust anyone and are always looking over their shoulder. They make it a point to always be aware of their surroundings and have a highly refined sense of detecting danger.

La Sombra is an expert at using the element of surprise. It gives him the upper hand when stalking his victims. He believes a good plan prevents piss poor performance in his lightning strikes against his enemies. La Sombra is pleased about being united with Atenco, his old friend. It gives him a purpose in life, more people to kill and also the ability to earn more money. With the extra money, he can now lavishly take care of his beloved mother who had slaved to take care of him.

La Sombra and the Barrio Maya gang have a large meal late in the afternoon in separate restaurants. Velarde eats with La Sombra and proudly reports his people are mentally ready and fully rested. They want to get it over with quickly and get back to El Paso with the tens of thousands of dollars they will each be paid. The money will all go to their girlfriends, booze, and drugs.

La Sombra tells Velarde, "Diga a los muchachos que vamos a salir del hotel a las once de la noche. Todos tienen que estar en sus posiciones antes de las tres de la mañana del Martes. Que aseguren que las radios operan." (Tell the boys that we will leave the hotel at eleven at night. Everybody has to be in position before three in the morning on Tuesday. Have them ensure the radios are operating.)

Velarde replies, "La Sombra, también les dije que no pueden ser detectados porque ponen en peligro el operativo. El asalto no se iniciará hasta que tu das la orden. El Cártel del Norte no sabrá que les pego. Que se jodan los cabrones." (La Sombra, I also told them they can't be detected because the operation will be endangered. The assault will not start until you give the order. The Cartel of the North will not know what hit them. Fuck the bastards.)

"Perfecto, nuestro plan no tiene margen para error. Ahora está en las manos de Jesús Malverde, el santo que nos protege. Él cuidará de nosotros, porque creemos en él. También fue de mi estado natal de Sinaloa." (Perfect, our plan doesn't have room for error. It is now in the hands of Jesus Malverde, the saint who protects us. He will take care of us because we believe in him. He is also from my home state of Sinaloa.)

Velarde knows that Malverde, the revered patron saint of Mexican drug traffickers, was a bandit who allegedly stole from the rich and gave to the poor. He had actually visited the shrine in Culiacan where ordinary people and criminals alike came to pray for favors. Traffickers asked Malverde to protect them from their enemies and also their valuable drug loads when they were being smuggled across the border into the U.S. Velarde had attended the annual May 3 celebration honoring Malverde. People would gather at midnight to wash themselves and the bust of Malverde in holy water. They brought offerings such as fine liquor, flowers, and candles. On the hood of a brightly decorated truck, they created a colorful altar with Malverde in the middle and marched proudly on the streets of the city. Some of the worshipers wore tattoos and medallions bearing Malverde's image on solid gold chains. Although, not recognized by the Catholic Church, the poor people admired him because he had rebelled against a corrupt government. Velarde was not a God fearing man and thought it was crazy to have a temple for someone who may have not even existed. *Oh well, to each his own*, he thought.

Later that evening, several vehicles transport the killers and their deadly tools of the trade. They stop a couple of miles from a Cartel of the North boss's house. They quickly unloaded their weapons and move silently into the shadows and tall brush. La Sombra and two men are dropped off at a greater distance from the area. It takes several minutes to carry the heavy machine gun up a small hill surrounded by several large pine trees. A few hours later, La Sombra conducts a communications check and is pleased everyone is in place. They settle in, watch and wait like a cat toying with a mouse until they are ready to pounce and spring their deadly ambush.

Later in the night, La Sombra lies on his back and looks up at the bright stars in the sky. He thinks about his life and the irony surrounding it. If his mother came from wealth, he probably would have become a doctor or a lawyer. Yet, destiny had decided he would follow another career path that was much more lucrative. He'd read many articles where journalists had described the drug trade as easy money. Such stupidity, he thought. They had no clue and didn't understand the risks involved in being a drug trafficker. It was a dangerous business seeped in violence and treachery. The life of a drug trafficker meant being not only the target of rival traffickers, but also of the military and police. It was an impossible situation,

La Sombra thought of the hypocrisy involved in their business because crooked politicians blatantly stole millions of dollars and were also paid by the cartels for protection. Yet, they denounced criminals and they were far worse than any of them.

La Sombra was of the strong opinion that it was better to live one year as a wealthy, feared criminal than a lifetime as a cowering dog living in the streets as a pauper. This was his motto and he would never change it. He vowed never to be taken alive and live in a cage for the rest of his life like a circus animal.

In the early morning hours, La Sombra and his team prepared their weapons and conducted another communications check. Everything was on track and now they just had to patiently wait for the Cartel of the North party scheduled for later that evening to begin. At noon, they ate flour tortillas, cheese, ham, and fresh jalapenos that they brought with them.

Everything tastes good when one is starved, thought El Sombra. He, however, would prefer a large steak with onions and potatoes. As he munches on his food, La Sombra surveys the area with a pair of powerful binoculars. He sees a large truck carrying a load of pigs squealing so loud, it's annoying to him. He also sees a couple of sedans zip by at a high rate of speed, but for the most part, traffic is minimal.

Later that afternoon, he contacts Atenco on the radio. They never use names and speak in code in the event their calls are being intercepted. The conversations are always less than five minutes long to avoid the triangulation of the communications, which would reveal their locations.

La Sombra reports, "Horale, estamos listos para la fiesta y todos los regalos serán entregados esta noche. Los niños se sorprenderán y explotarán de alegría. Voy a enviar sus saludos y profundo pesar que no pudo asistir personalmente." (Hey, we're ready for the party and all the gifts will be delivered tonight. The children will be surprised and explode with joy. I will send your greetings and deep regret that you could not attend in person.)

"Me alegro de que todo está bien y espero que los niños disfruten de todos los juguetes que traen. Déjame saber cómo va cuando se ha terminado. Cuídate." (I am glad that everything is fine and hope the kids enjoy all the toys you bring. Let me know how it went when it's over. Take care.)

La Sombra closes his eyes and tries to take a catnap, but a load of adrenaline is coursing through his nervous system. He knows he has become addicted to the adrenaline rush brought by the thrill of the hunt and the killing of people. The more violent the killings are, the higher the rush. He can hardly wait for the action to begin. He drinks more water, then pisses against one of the trees and wishes he were pissing on the entire Cartel of the North. He sits back down and settles into a deadly calm.

When the sun fades over the horizon it is replaced by a full moon, which provides some visibility. It is early evening when several black Mercedes SUV's and sedans begin to arrive at the house. The Barrio Maya gang members positioned in front of the house estimate at least fifty men. A short time later a large mariachi group arrives in a van and begin to unload their musical instruments. They're dressed in traditional charro outfits with colorful Mexican sombreros. The last to arrive are five cars full of prostitutes with glittery short skirts, high heels, and revealing blouses. They laugh loudly among themselves and quickly enter the house. Four men armed with AK-47's are positioned near the front door, but no security is placed in back of the residence. The guards smoke cigarettes and talk among themselves without a care in the world. Soon, the sound of loud music can be heard. It is the song made famous by Jose Alfredo Jimenez named El Rey (The King):

"Yo sé bien que estoy afuera; pero el dia en que yo me muera sé que tendras que llorar Llorar y llorar;

Llorar y llorar; Diras que no me quisiste;

Pero vas a estar muy triste y asi te vas a quedar;

Con dinero y sin dinero; hago siempre lo que quiero;

Y mi palabra es la ley; no tengo trono ni reina;

Ni nadie que me comprenda; pero sigo siendo el rey."

(I know very well that I'm out [of your life]; but the day I die I know you'll have to cry and cry and cry;

Cry and cry; you may say you never loved me; but you're going to be really sad; and that's how you're going to stay;

With or without money; I always do what I want;

and my words are the law; I have neither a throne nor a queen; nor anyone that understands me; but I remain the king.)

An hour after the party is in full swing. Velarde clicks on his radio at a very low volume and whispers to La Sombra. "Parece que todo el mundo está aquí. Quieres que nosotros empezamos a matar a estos perros?" (It seems that everyone is here. Do you want us to start killing these dogs?)

La Sombra replies, "Adelante." (Lets do it.)

The two snipers across the road from the house put the first two men in their crosshairs and slowly pull the trigger. The close distance made them easy targets. They quickly set their sights on the other two men and in less than five seconds all four lay crumpled on the ground. They never knew what hit them. Next RPG's are almost simultaneously launched from the front and the rear of the house. They penetrate the walls like a sword through air. The lethal blasts literally shook the foundation of the house. Another two RPG's are fired and two of the walls are almost completely disintegrated. Smoke and fire begin to appear accompanied by a chorus of penetrating screams. Two men attempt to run out the back door, but are quickly cut down by a spray of lead from an AK-47. The assault team then approaches the house and finds the Cartel of the North regional boss severely wounded on the floor in the main living room. Blood is pouring from his legs and head. He looks up and knows what is coming. He begs for his life. Velarde grabs him by his long black hair and pulls an eight-inch military dagger from the back of his waistband. With one swift motion, Velarde decapitates him and a thick arterial spray of blood shoots into the air like a geyser. Velarde carries the head to the front of the house and impales it on a decorative spear on the white wrought iron fence. The head is full of blood and the eyes and mouth are wide open in horror.

Moments later, La Sombra is told by radio that three blue and white policia estatal (state police) cars are on the road heading in his direction at a high rate of speed. La Sombra figures someone who saw the house on fire and or heard the thunderous explosions notified them. He is aware the state police in Chihuahua are bought and paid for by the Cartel of the North. He is now going to pay them as well, but not with silver---with lead. He is ready and can see the bright headlights in the distance. As the three cars approach, La Sombra opens up with the heavy machine gun and the bright tracers streak rapidly across the night like swarms of angry bees. The high caliber bullets find their mark and easily tear through metal and rip huge chunks of flesh from the bodies of the policemen inside. Body parts, arms, legs, torsos, and heads slam against the interior of the car and some flew out of the cars onto the side of the road. The machine gun's continuous blasting is ear shattering, but doesn't faze La Sombra. Eventually, the hot lead penetrates the gas tanks and the cars explode into huge balls of fire. The twelve state police officers don't feel the intense heat. They are already dead.

La Sombra then calmly speaks into his radio and orders his drivers to pick everyone up so they can leave the area. Once the weapons are rapidly loaded, La Sombra meets Velarde in front of the house and both put up a Narco Manta (Narco message)--- which they prepare on a large white sheet with bright red lettering, blood on pure white. It said:

SOY JOSÉ ATENCO Y EL TERROR DE LOS PERROS DEL CARTEL DEL NORTE QUE ROBAN DE LAS BOCAS

*DE LOS POBRES. ELLOS TRABAJAN CON EL GO-
BIERNO CORRUPTO DE MIERDA. TRAEMOS MUERTE
A TODOS LOS QUE APOYAN A ESTOS BASTARDOS.
SOMOS MIEMBROS DEL PODEROSO CÁRTEL ALI-
ANZA DE SANGRE.*"

(I am Jose Atenco, the terror of the dogs from the Cartel of
the North who steal from the mouths of the poor. They
work with the corrupt government of shit. We bring death
to all who support these bastards. We are members of the
powerful *Blood Alliance Cartel*.)

La Sombra and Velarde take one last look at the bloody
carnage they have inflicted. Blood is actually flowing in
small streams from the house as it burns. That night, they
snuffed out at least fifty lives. *Not bad for a day's work*,
thought La Sombra. The violent assassins with their arsenal
of weapons drive rapidly southbound as flames lick the sky
in their rearview mirrors.

La Sombra calls Atenco, "José, todos los perros y sus putas ya no existen. Escupo sobre de todos ellos." (José, all the
dogs and their whores no longer exist. I spit on them all.")

"Bien, mi viejo amigo. Tenga cuidado. Yo espero su regreso para celebrar esta victoria. Lo hiciste bien." (Good, my
old friend. Be careful, I wait for your return so we can celebrate this victory. You did well.)

CHAPTER
6

Crystal Powder

Villa sits impatiently at a large brown rectangular conference table on the fifth floor of the U.S. Embassy waiting for the Ambassador to arrive. All of the other agencies have representatives present for the daily meeting that usually lasts about an hour. Everyone is dressed in heavily starched white shirts, dark suits, and conservative ties. All except Villa who likes bright Jerry Garcia ties. There are no women at the table. It is definitely a Boys Club.

The purpose of the meetings is to brief the current Ambassador, James Stiles, of each agencies' current and future plans. Moving quickly with purpose, Stiles enters the room and quickly sits at the head of the table. He frowns as his gaze falls on each man.

Finally, he speaks, "I am exceptionally concerned about the expanding levels of corruption within the Mexican government. Your reports are quite clear about this issue." Stiles pauses a moment for effect, and then goes on, "Even more disconcerting is the recent communiqué from the CIA exposing corruption within Los Pinos." (It is Mexico's version of the White House). He states that it appears the Mexican President and most of his Cabinet are involved in receiving kickbacks from several companies that were recently awarded billions of dollars in construction contracts. He also mentions that the Minister of Defense is receiving bribes for protection from the Blood Alliance Cartel. He talks about a military operation in which the army reported killing twenty-five drug traffickers at an isolated ranch in Veracruz.

According to a spokesperson, the army had come under fire as they approached the ranch. Allegedly, the firefight had lasted several hours until each one of the traffickers was killed. Information from several sources, including from soldiers that were there, revealed that none of the men who were killed had weapons. It was a disturbing violation of human rights, which were reoccurring over and over again. The Ambassador is on a roll and he is more than pissed at the Mexican government. He feels they are giving him nothing but lip service and it has started to annoy and frustrate him.

He then launches into a tirade about the Merida Initiative, a security agreement between the U.S. and Mexico/Central America, to counter the threats of drug trafficking and money laundering. Red faced with anger, the Ambassador says that he is very close to immediately halting the initiative and no longer providing Mexico with training, equipment, and intelligence. He mentions that more than twenty-five billion dollars are flowing from the U.S. into the country, which are proceeds from the drug trade. After burning hot for a while, Stiles begins to cool down. Then he starts to lecture everyone.

He says, "Unfortunately, the problem is much more complex and is driven by the huge consumption and demand in the United States. Furthermore, I figure that over sixty million people in Mexico live in extreme poverty. As a result, they have three options for survival: migration; dangerous work in the local economy; and crime. The end result is that drug traffickers find easy pickings amongst the poor. We have provided more than one and a half billion dollars under the Merida Initiative and not a single dime is dedicated to prevention or rehabilitation. I am also worried that about ninety percent of the weapons used by the Mexican cartels originate from our country. I guess it is a much broader issue and the U.S. is not entirely clean on this matter."

No one wants to prolong the meeting so everyone keeps the briefings to a minimum with the exception of the nerdy chief of the commerce section who rambles on regarding the status of the North American Free Trade Agreement. He explains the agreement between the U.S., Mexico, and Canada designed to allow goods and services to move more freely is working according to plan. He lets out a loud sigh, adding that drug traffickers are now using the trade pact to smuggle large amounts of drugs into the U.S.

With a look of absolute dejection, he says that during the previous year almost five million commercial vehicles had crossed into the U.S. from Mexico. Unfortunately, only one out of twenty vehicles is searched because U.S. Customs agents were overwhelmed and didn't have the resources to search them all.

Villa can almost see tears forming in the eyes of the meek little man. He thinks of approaching him afterwards and recommending that he invest in a good bottle of tequila for medicinal purposes, but it will probably only make matters worse. He might have continued his discussion on NAFTA and Villa doesn't have the time or inclination to listen to him. Villa is keenly aware of the competing interests within the embassy, but makes no mistake that trade and economic policies are first and foremost. He knows they are important, however, shortsighted since the violent and expansionistic trends of the powerful drug cartels are beginning to strangle the Mexican economy like a large, powerful anaconda.

As a DEA agent, Villa knows all the odds are in favor of the criminals and their sophisticated networks, which have flourished under the dominant Revolutionary Institutional Party known as the PRI. They have controlled Mexican politics for seventy-one consecutive years and allowed the cartels to grow in exchange for hundreds of millions of dollars in bribes. Greed has overcome every other consideration such as professional integrity and concern for the general well-being of the country.

The cartels dominate vast territories, police forces, public officials and those who resist are quickly sent to an unmarked grave. Villa knows that pursuing the cartels is a hazardous business because they have placed themselves above the law and will kill anyone on a whim. Making matters more complicated is the protection they are afforded at all levels of the government. The corruption is rampant, which contributes to the wholesale violence wreaking havoc throughout the country.

In order to have an impact, Villa is also aware he will have to weave his way through the numerous political landmines to get to the cartel leaders and their infrastructure. He spends many sleepless nights formulating strategies and methods of overcoming obstacles that will surface during operations and investigations. Villa doesn't believe in status quo. He pursues comprehensive and dynamic strategies coupled with innovative tactics. To him, status quo is for losers who have no vision or are just plain lazy.

He also doesn't suffer the fools who are promoted because of nothing more than the color of their skin or belong to the cliques that control the DEA. Villa abhors the discrimination that occurs within the agency and the fact that most minorities have to work much harder and accomplish a lot more in order to advance in their careers.

Unfortunately, this didn't always ensure advancement within the agency. Villa is gratified by the fact that most minorities serve on the front lines and in the trenches against some of the most brutal traffickers in the world. They are proud of their service and didn't spend their time with self-promotion or hiding behind their desks. Villa also sees many who spend their time sucking up to get promotions. People who sell their integrity and lower themselves in such a despicable manner disgusts him. He believes if you can't achieve it through merit, you should not expect any reward.

Villa calls Ventura and makes arrangements to meet him for dinner at the *Rincon Argentino*. The restaurant is their favorite and it is known for its beautiful interior and its exquisite cuts of beef. The ceiling is painted to resemble the sky and a thatched roof covers the bar. The dining area reminds Villa of a beautifully appointed lodge. It has the best steaks in the city, with eight different cuts and a wide selection of Argentinian wines.

Two months earlier, both friends had been at the restaurant when they spotted six gunmen belonging to the Cartel of the North sitting at a nearby table. Villa recognized them from wanted posters and photos in a DEA investigative file on the cartel. The gunmen were engrossed in conversation and had several bottles of expensive wine on the table. Villa noticed one of them had a pistol slightly sticking out of his pocket. Villa and Ventura had just started enjoying their oversized *bife de chorizo* (ribeye) steaks and decided to eat them before approaching the cartel assassins. Besides, they could keep an eye on them and there was no reason to prematurely spoil a quiet evening and a great meal.

After gorging themselves on the delicious meat and having one last glass of red wine, Villa and Ventura approached the group and pointed their semi-automatic handguns at them. The thugs looked surprised and didn't immediately follow instructions to put their hands behind their heads. Ventura struck the closest one to him on the head with the butt of his weapon and knocked him out. He fell onto the floor with a thud and blood pouring from his wound formed a small red pool on the floor. The others quickly obeyed and were placed on their knees next to their friend. A search revealed all of them were armed and were packing extra magazines filled with hollow point bullets. Many of the patrons panicked and fled the restaurant like bats out of hell. The waiters quickly moved away from the area in terror expecting a wild gunfight to erupt in the middle of the dining area. Ventura had some of his men who were outside transport the cartel gunmen to one of the local jails. Villa and Ventura went back to their table and had a shot of tequila to finish the evening.

Now, once again, back at the *Rincon Argentino*, Villa tells his friend he hopes the evening will be much quieter than the last time. They chuckle and Ventura looks around and says the men in the restaurant are too old to pull the trigger, much less lift a handgun. Villa roars with laughter and the elderly couple at a nearby table glare at them with disdain.

The conversation is light and both Ventura and Villa enjoy each other's company and in every sense, except genetically, they are brothers. They can discuss personal problems and seek advice on anything that crosses their minds. They begin to discuss the bureaucrats within their respective agencies who are completely useless. They are more concerned about their careers than carrying out their responsibilities. Villa and Ventura believe they can easily be sidestepped because they are so stupid. Their friendship has now become so close they will do anything for one another, including taking a bullet.

As with all their conversations, it eventually shifts to work related issues. Villa tells Ventura that Atenco has now become the primary source for methamphetamine in the U.S. The addiction rates and overdose deaths were rapidly increasing, especially in the western part of the country. Despite intensified efforts by law enforcement, it is surpassing cocaine as the drug of choice. It is a powerful stimulant and is cheap and easy to make. Methamphetamine is being called the poor man's cocaine.

Ventura nods his head and waves his arms as he acknowledges what Villa is saying. He quietly talks about how corruption, at all levels of the Mexican government, is making

the drug trade an insidious problem. Ventura says his beloved country is in a state of crisis and if things plunge
deeper into the abyss of the corrosive drug trade, it can literally become a failed state. He laments that drug money is
corrupting high-level officials and manipulating local, state,
and even national elections. It is used to buy more sophisticated weapons and generate even more criminal activity. In
a sad voice, he continues by saying that foreign investors are
steering clear of Mexico because of the instability. He says
that it is also having a major disruptive impact on tourism.
Ventura explains that many financial institutions in Mexico
are laundering hundreds of millions of dollars each year. He
calls it financial insurgency. He says that Mexico and the
U.S. have a love/hate relationship because Mexico sends
drugs north and the U.S. sends them weapons in return. He
smiles and quotes the former Mexican dictator, Porfirio
Diaz, who said, *"Poor Mexico, so far from God and so close
to the United States."* Both Villa and Ventura break out in
laughter.

After having yet another memorable evening, both walk
out of the restaurant with their digestive systems in full over-
drive. Ventura's men are outside and quickly drive up and
open the door for their boss. Villa makes the lonely drive
home along the brightly lit streets with the usual heavy traffic. While at the office the next day, Villa is still uncomfortable with the huge steak he ate the previous evening. He is
convinced it will take a week to fully digest it and is on the
verge of walking to a nearby pharmacy to buy something that
will relieve his indigestion when he receives a call from Bob
Mange. The static on the line makes it difficult to hear so he
tells Mange he will call him back right away. Villa has Ur-

sula make the call and it takes several tries because it is always difficult to make international calls from Mexico. Villa finds it very frustrating not having reliable and trustworthy communications, which is so critical to operations. Finally, the call goes through and the line is now much clearer.

Mange is more cheerful than usual, "Hey Miguel, I have some good news. The German federal police in Stuttgart just called and said someone allegedly representing Quimicas Mexico has just put in an order with ChemCon for three tons of ephedrine. The person apparently identified himself as Antonio Gallegos and said he would wire transfer the full payment in a few days."

"That is good news indeed. I want the load to proceed to Mexico, but we must track it once it enters the country. We need to identify the lab being used to convert the ephedrine to meth. No later than tomorrow, I will send a couple of my best technical experts to Stuttgart with several transponders that they will place in some of the barrels. I'll need assistance from your end to support the techies."

"Ok, but it is going to cost you a dinner at the finest Italian restaurant the next time we meet."

Villa laughs, "Oh well, nothing in life is free, right?"

"Have your guys call me once they have their reservations and I will have a couple of my agents pick them up at the airport and take them to ChemCon. I will arrange everything. Have a good day and stay safe."

Shortly afterwards, Villa has a meeting with Danny Baxter who was one of the best technical experts in the agency. He has placed hundreds of transponders on trafficker aircraft and boats, which have led to large seizures and arrests in the U.S. and several foreign countries. Baxter reminds Villa of a country western singer. He has long reddish hair and a well-trimmed beard. He likes to wear ostrich boots and loves colorful western shirts. Villa likes him because of his great personality and *Can Do* attitude.

"Danny, I just got a call from Bob Mange in Germany. He said that a rep from the fictitious company Quimicas Mexico has ordered three tons of ephedrine, obviously to be processed into high-grade meth. I need you to fly out tomorrow with some transponders and please take as many of your people as you need. It will be a rush job, but you will have support from our guys in Germany. They will take you wherever you need to go, and help you with anything else you need."

"Not a problem. I will take two of my guys and start packing some transponders, cabling, and other things we will need. This will be a fucking great operation if we can pull it off. I can feel my adrenaline pumping already. I live for this shit."

Within hours, Baxter and his team have packed three TAM-212 rechargeable satellite transponders into secure black metal cases. The TAM-212 is ideal since it doesn't need an external power source and is contained in a small compact package. It uses a disposable lithium battery and can be used for extended tracking periods of up to five years. It has magnetic feet with screw attachments, giving greater flexibility to monitor moving or fixed targets.

Miguel sits at his large desk and smiles. He knows that most people were unaware that it only takes three spy satellites to blanket the world. Space is, however, cluttered with military, CIA, and civilian satellites. The capabilities of the satellites used by the military and CIA are mind-boggling and can penetrate cloud cover to monitor geographical areas and human targets. Villa is very familiar with this technology and also knows that NASA is the sole agency that launches them from Cape Kennedy in Florida or Vandenberg Air Force base in California. He thinks to himself that advances in technology has been nothing short of miraculous. If used properly, they provide a great advantage in tracking criminals and terrorists across the globe.

The next day, Villa calls Mange and tells him about the flight and arrival times of Baxter and his team in Stuttgart.

"Great! My people will be waiting for them. ChemCon will allow your guys to place the transponders in a private area where they can work and not be observed by nosy employees. They will also give them a copy of the invoice."

"Thanks Bob, I really appreciate all your help. I will be in touch."

A few minutes later, Villa takes the small elevator to the fifth floor of the embassy where the offices of the CIA are located. The tall, skinny female receptionist recognizes him and escorts him to Station Chief Les Tool's office located down a long, narrow hallway. Red lights are turned on and flash brightly. This is their way of alerting CIA personnel that someone not belonging to the agency is in their office. Several conservatively dressed men and women pass in the hallway and look suspiciously at Villa. *The CIA culture has reached one of complete paranoia*, he thinks silently.

The receptionist sticks her head in the door and says,

"Mr. Villa is here to see you, Mr. Tool."

"How are you, Miguel? Please come in." Tool is a tall, lanky man with curly hair. He has been in charge of the CIA office in Mexico for several years after serving a long tour in Afghanistan. He had been wounded in both legs with shrapnel during an attack on the embassy in Kabul. He is down to earth and not stiff like a three-day-old tortilla like most of his brethren.

"Les, we have an ops taking place and I need some support in tracking a load of ephedrine that is coming to Mexico very soon. The precursor is coming from Germany and we feel that it is going to one of Atenco's super labs somewhere in the country where it will be converted into meth. I have our techies in Germany placing hidden transponders in the shipment so we can track it. We need one of your satellites to monitor the transponder signals so we can follow it into Mexico and then ultimately to the lab."

"Miguel, all our satellites are tied up watching the situation in Syria and Iraq, especially now with ISIS gaining momentum in the region. We spent tons of money training the Iraqi military and they retreat from a bunch of fucking Islamic radicals driving 1980 Toyota pickup trucks. It's fucking unbelievable. I can probably get my hands on one of the National Reconnaissance Office's (NRO) satellites. I am sure you have used them before. They are now one of sixteen intelligence agencies that we have in the U.S. They are based in Chantilly, Virginia. The NRO has some of the best overhead reconnaissance systems in the world. Actually, one of their surveillance systems is better than ours, a much more sophisticated model with super advanced technology. It is the NROL-39 satellite, which was launched a couple of years ago. It is so highly classified I shouldn't even be *mentioning* it much less talking about it. The head of the NRO called me a couple of days ago wanting a viable operational mission to support. They'll be excited to work on an international drug case. They seem bored and really need some adrenaline flowing through their clogged veins. I will take care of it for you. Just let me know the transponder codes and we will be in business."

"Perfect! I will get back to you as soon as I hear from my guys in Germany. Thanks for the help."

As Villa leaves the CIA offices, he sees the annoying red lights go off. Maybe, I will put sirens in the DEA offices and turn them on when we have visitors, he thinks to himself and smiles as he pictures the humorous scenario.

The following day, Mange calls Villa and his voice is upbeat. "Miguel, I have been in contact with Baxter in Stuttgart and he wants to let you know they are moving right along with installing the transponders. They placed and anchored them at the bottom of three random barrels. In order to fully conceal them, they put a thin metal plate on top and sealed it with a welder's torch. Soon they will fill them with the ephedrine powder. They will never be found among the hundreds of barrels.

"Thanks for keeping me abreast of the progress,"

"That is not all, ChemCon told us that they received a call allegedly from an employee at Quimicas Mexico and they want the ephedrine to be transported by ground to the seaport in Antwerp. Upon arrival, it will be loaded to a coastal freighter named *Santa Fe* that is registered to the Mexican company."

"The spooks (CIA) are going to get us satellite support so we can follow the ship and transponder signals. Bob, what can you tell me about the Antwerp port."

"Miguel, it is one of the largest seaports in Europe. Belgium has made huge capital investments on it and is working to expand its capabilities. We have several informants at the port who provide us with information on drug smuggling through there."

"Please have Baxter send me the transponder frequencies by the end of the day. I need to pass them to the three-letter agency as soon as possible. See if you can have your informants get any information on the ship, its crew, and departure date… I guess this will mean more lunches and dinners that I will owe you."

"Miguel, you don't have enough money to pay me for all the favors. It's a good thing we work for the same agency."

"I guess so, especially with your freaking appetite. Thanks again, buddy."

Villa begins to research and plot the timeline for the shipment of ephedrine from Stuttgart to Antwerp by land. He determines the distance is about three hundred forty-three miles and will take about a six-hour drive to arrive at the seaport. Next, he calculates a distance of slightly over six thousand nautical miles between Antwerp and Veracruz. At ten knots per hour, it will take the Santa Fe about twenty-five days to make the trip. This gives him valuable data so he can plan his strategy and timelines. He also knows, based on his experience, that once the ephedrine is loaded on the Santa Fe, the barrels will be mislabeled as something else to facilitate its entry into Mexico.

Later that evening, Villa calls Ventura and gives him an update of the operation. He also requests that Ventura tap the telephone lines of the Mexican Customs office in Veracruz as soon as possible. He is interested in identifying the corrupt officials involved with facilitating the movement of ephedrine through the port. He also tells Ventura to intercept the cell phone of the Customs official who signed the paperwork on the last shipment of ephedrine.

"I'll get some of my men to get it done. I should just get our Navy to blow up the fucking ship as it enters Mexico's territorial waters."

"I know how you feel, but we need to locate the lab and arrest the corrupt officials in Veracruz."

"You are right. I just get frustrated with the situation sometimes."

"Ok, my friend, we will talk soon.

Villa understands Ventura's frustration. It is difficult to swallow that drug traffickers are greedy and power hungry thugs who sometimes get away with murder. They have absolutely no concern for the suffering and death caused by their reprehensible and irresponsible behaviors. It is also frustrating to risk one's life to capture some of the worst killers in the world and then have corrupt officials set them free to continue preying on society. Money drives the entire process and everyone is only concerned about themselves and not the well being of others. Villa is disgusted with the drug consumption in his country, which causes epidemic addiction, corruption, terrorism, and violence. They, too, were only concerned about getting high and are now pushing for the legalization of drugs. He compares the struggle against illegal drugs to standing in the middle of a hurricane with a little cocktail umbrella. Regardless, he knows it is a calling and he and his band of brothers will continue to struggle for their respective countries and save as many people as possible.

Baxter calls later that day, "Miguel, everything is done and I will send you the transponder frequencies through secure fax. We checked all of the transponders and they are working perfectly. All we have to do now is track them to their final destination. Through the signals, we can also determine the route of the ship via satellite. The agents here will take photos of the freighter before it leaves Antwerp. The guys and I will be leaving here tomorrow.

"Thanks for the great work, Danny. Pass my regards to the guys and thank them for me."

"Will do and see you soon."

Later that day, after receiving the transponder codes, Villa pays the CIA a visit and catches Tool leaving his office. Tool is in a rumpled dark suit with a loud green tie. It looks like he had been sleeping on a park bench. He is heading to a meeting with a contact in the Mexican army.

He smiles and says, "Miguel, I was going to call you later today and let you know the satellite coverage you need will happen. The NRO became even more excited when I told them it involved Atenco."

"That is really good news. He hands Tool the codes. You can pass these to the NRO. Thanks again."

Villa goes back to his office and relaxes a few minutes. The coordination of investigations and operations in foreign countries is intense and involves a large number of players, much more so than working in the U.S. Most headquarters staff has never served abroad and they don't understand the complexities involved in carrying out a successful operation. Rather, they try to downplay working in foreign environments only because they lack this valuable experience. Moreover, all the top drug traffickers in the world operate on foreign soil. They are the top tier sources of supply. The traffickers in the U.S. are further down in the food chain.

Rafael Ochoa drives his brown Toyota Land Cruiser rapidly down the rugged, winding dirt road in the forbidding Sierra Madre Mountains between the states of Sinaloa and

Durango. Huge clouds of dust lift into the air from the dry earth and the vehicle bounces violently up and down. He finally reaches an isolated cabin surrounded by an army of heavily armed men who point their menacing AK-47s at the vehicle, but quickly lower them when they recognize him. Ochoa is taller than most Mexicans and has black hair combed over to the side. His blue jeans are almost brown with dust and his boots are well worn and their color has faded long ago.

Ochoa slowly gets out of the truck and yells, "Pinches carreteras están peor cada día. Mi espalda me está matando a la chingada. Tengo que hablar con Atenco." (Fucking roads are worse every day. My back is fucking killing me. I have to talk to Atenco.) One of the guards wearing a white cowboy hat nods his head for him to enter the house.

Ochoa climbs the wooden stairs to the front door and trips on the last one falling on his face. He moans and rolls over on his back, still in shock and completely disoriented. He doesn't break his nose, but blood begins to spurt from it. He finally gets on his feet and walks in the door. Atenco sees him and begins to laugh.

"Qué coño esta pasado? Porqué tu novia sigue golpeado a usted? Estas jodido." (What the fuck happened to you? Why is your girlfriend still hitting you? You are fucked.)

Atenco roars at his own comments, which causes his bodyguards to also laugh. They dared not laugh at Atenco's jokes. Failure to honor Atenco's humor could prove fatal. Ochoa also laughs and sits on the table and is given tissues to wipe the blood from his nose. He sees La Sombra standing nearby staring at him. It makes him perspire and he becomes visibly nervous. He begins to involuntarily pump his right leg rapidly up and down. He thinks that La Sombra doesn't respect him and looks right through him as though he didn't exist.

Ochoa begins, "Senor Atenco, vine a decirle en persona que el envío de la efedrina se ha ordenado y estara en el puerto de Antwerp en los próximos dos días. Nuestro barco, el Santa Fe, va estar en espera para cargarlo. Desembarca tan pronto como se preparan los documentos necesarios, y debe llegar en el Puerto de Veracruz, en veinticinco días más o menos. En ese momento todo el etiquetado se habrá cambiado para que parezca que se trata de material utilizado para fabricar cosméticos. Estamos en comunicación con nuestros contactos de Aduanas en Veracruz para que estén pendientes de que no tenemos problemas." (Mr. Atenco, I came to tell you in person that the shipment of ephedrine has been ordered and will be in the port of Antwerp in the next two days. Our ship, the Santa Fe, will be waiting there to be loaded. It will depart as soon as the necessary documents are prepared and should arrive in the port of Veracruz in about twenty-five days or so. By that time the labeling will have been changed to make it appear that it is material used to manufacture cosmetics. We are in touch with our contacts in Customs at Veracruz who are on standby so we don't have problems.)

"Esas son buenas noticias. Tiene todo preparado en el laboratorio? Tenemos que convertirlo a cristal tan pronto como sea posible. Como ustedes saben, estamos en guerra con los perros del Cartel del Norte. Parte del dinero se utilizará para ampliar el número de sicarios que tenemos en la calle. Quiero enviar algunos a la zona de Chihuahua a matar a todos asociados con la gente de Romero. También se recogerá información para nosotros." (That's good news. Do you have everything prepared in the laboratory? We have to convert it to crystal meth as soon as possible. As you know, we are at war with the dogs from the Cartel of the North. Some of the money will be used to expand the number of hitmen we have on the street. I also want to send some to the area of Chihuahua to kill anyone associated with Romero's people. They can also collect information for us.)

Ochoa quickly responds, "Sí señor, estamos preparados en el laboratorio principal y tengo cinco químicos que utilizaremos. Están esperando la llamada de nosotros. Usted tendrá que darme algunas personas para proporcionar seguridad a la hora de empezar el proceso de conversión. Hice un inventario reciente sobre todos los productos químicos que necesitaremos. Tenemos un montón de acetona, ácido clorhídrico, amoniaco anhidro y éter." (Yes sir, we are prepared at the principal laboratory and have five chemists we use. They are waiting for the call from us. You have to give me some people to provide security when we start the conversion process. I made a recent inventory of all the chemicals we need. We do have a lot of acetone, hydrochloric acid, anhydrous ammonia and ether.)

Atenco looks at La Sombra, "Cuando llegue el momento, envia a Ochoa algunos de nuestros mejores sicarios para proteger nuestro laboratorio. Desafortunadamente, ahora no sólo tenemos que preocuparnos por la maldita DEA y los federales, sino también el Cartel del Norte. Estamos rodeados de enemigos. También dé la orden, yo no quiero que nadie use sus teléfonos celulares dentro de cincuenta kilómetros de mí. Es demasiado fácil para rastrear y localizar a mí con la tecnología que tienen los gringos." (When the time comes, send Ochoa some of our best assassins to protect our laboratory. Unfortunately, we not only have to worry about the fucking DEA and feds, but also the Cartel of the

North. Enemies surround us. Also give the order, I do not want anyone to use cell phones within fifty kilometers of me. It is too easy to track and locate me with the technology the gringos have.)

Ochoa speaks, "Señor, Es muy difícil comunicarse en persona cada vez que tenemos que pasar información." (Sir, it is very difficult to communicate in person every time we have to pass information.)

Atenco thought for a moment and then responds, "Tienes razón. He investigado posibles teléfonos celulares encriptados, pero ellos también pueden ser interceptados y situado a través de la tecnología GPS. Voy a tener algunos de nuestros hombres con radios y teléfonos en un pueblo cercano que está a punto de sesenta kilómetros de aquí y los utilizan como un sistema de retransmisión de mensajes. Ellos tomarán la información y luego manejar aquí para pasarlo en persona." (You are right. I researched possible encrypted cell phones, but they can also be intercepted and located through GPS technology. I'll have some of our men with radios and telephones in a nearby village that is about sixty kilometers from here and use them as a message relay system. They will take the information and then drive here to pass it in person.)

"Esa es una muy buena idea y ahorrará mucho tiempo. Bueno, yo voy a salir, a menos que tenga más instrucciones para mí. Voy a seguir informando sobre la operación." (That's a very good idea and it will save time. Well, I'm leaving, unless you have further instructions for me. I will continue to report on the operation.)

"Eso está bien. Lo dejo en sus manos para asegurarse de que todo salga bien. No podemos tener ningún hilos sueltos." (That's fine. I leave it in your hands to make sure everything goes well. We cannot have any loose threads.)

Ochoa quickly jumps into his Land Cruiser and drives away at a high rate of speed. His foot heavily pushes down on the accelerator. He feels relieved to leave the area. He considers himself a businessman, but knew he was playing with his life since Atenco and his associates could decide, at any time, to kill him on nothing more than the pleasure of watching him die. Like everyone in the drug business, he was a gambler playing against the odds on the roulette wheel of death. He swallows hard and thinks to himself, *it is what it is.* He slams his foot on the gas to drive even faster as if the Grim Reaper himself was chasing him down the road.

After being notified of the Santa Fe's departure from Antwerp, Villa gets a phone call from Ventura. It is the news he has been waiting for. Ventura says that his men have been intercepting all the calls made by Customs employees at the port in Veracruz and there is no doubt most of them are on the take. During the last three days, calls had intensified regarding the tons of ephedrine that are en route. Ventura's agents have broken the code words being used when they communicated with one another. They referred to the precursor chemicals as *Familia* (family) and the Santa Fe as *La Santa* (The Saint). They also use the code name of *La Compañía* (The Company) to refer to the Blood Alliance Cartel.

Ventura is pleased with the valuable information that is being collected through the wire intercepts. He said his men are also conducting physical surveillance of the Customs officials who are seen having regular meetings with members of the Blood Alliance Cartel at different restaurants. Obviously, they are busy coordinating the entry of the ephedrine into Mexico. Dealing with the Blood Alliance Cartel means that no mistakes will be tolerated and killing Customs agents means nothing to Atenco. Villa thanks his friend for the information.

Constant communication between Villa and the CIA continue in tracking the Santa Fe and another two weeks pass when it is determined it is fast approaching Veracruz. The situation will soon be reaching critical mass with cops and criminals each planning to thwart the other. Villa and Ventura know they will have to be more ruthless and cunning than the traffickers. It comes easy for them since they are both alpha males on steroids.

Villa is very familiar with the seaport in Veracruz. It is Mexico's principal port on the Atlantic side. He also knows it is used regularly by traffickers to bring precursors used in the manufacture of heroin and methamphetamine from Europe. The depth of the water is about thirty-five feet and therefore can accommodate most ships. Additionally, it has powerful commercial lifts that can off-load shipments of over a hundred tons.

The following afternoon, Tool tells Villa that the Santa Fe has arrived and is on one of the docks. An hour later, Ventura calls and also confirms its arrival. Villa tells him to continue the wiretaps and surveillance at the port, but not to take any action that will heat things up. Villa says the satellite will continue tracking the precursors when they are transported from the port.

The next morning, Ventura calls and tells Villa his men watched as a single maritime container was lifted from the hold of the Santa Fe and hoisted onto the flatbed of a tractor trailer rig, which immediately left the area. They also see several Customs officials on the wharf, but the container didn't undergo any type of inspection, which is required by

Mexican law. Villa tells him not to arrest them until the clandestine lab is located and seized. Ventura says he will pass the word to his men immediately. Before hanging up, Villa makes arrangements to meet with Ventura at Sanborn's restaurant near the U.S. Embassy. Meantime, the CIA begins passing hourly coordinates on the location of the precursors. They are being transported in a westerly direction from Veracruz and the truck is moving at about seventy miles an hour.

A short time later, Villa meets Ventura at the restaurant and they order a couple of pork tortas (sandwiches) and begin to fine tune their operational strategy. Ventura has twenty agents in cars following the truck carrying the precursors at a safe distance since they had decided to let the satellite do the tracking. Regardless, it is important to position a large group of agents close to where the operation will take place. Ventura also has four Bell 212 helicopters ready to transport others from Mexico City and then use them to direct ground units from the air in the event of a firefight or as traffickers attempted to escape as the operation unfolded. Mexican marines would also provide support during the raid. Villa mentions it is critical to ensure that the lab is operational and in the process of converting the ephedrine into meth before they moved in. Otherwise, the charges against the traffickers would amount to nothing more than a slap on the wrist. Besides, time is on their side since it will take days to process even a small portion of the precursors to meth. The next set of coordinates from the satellite indicated that the truck is still headed west and traveling through the state of Mexico

Late that evening, the truck enters the state of Colima, which borders the Pacific Ocean. Two hours later, the satellite indicates the coordinates remain static. The truck has stopped, hopefully at its final destination. The final coordinates are 19"19'41"N103"36'10"W. Villa plots them on a large map and determines that the location is Cuauhtemoc, Colima. It is an ideal area for a clandestine lab since it was sparsely populated with little government presence in the area. The population is less than ten thousand and people there have little regard for the central government and never provide any information.

In the morning, Villa arrives at the embassy and immediately goes to the CIA office to meet with Tool. The CIA chief is sitting at his desk with a large cup of steaming coffee and a plate of colorful Mexican cookies. He pulls out a folder marked Top Secret and hands it to Villa. It contains satellite photos of the location where the ephedrine has been taken. It shows a ranch with a small, rustic house and a very large barn behind it. A herd of cows are seen grazing on tall grass. Also, eight pick-up trucks and SUVs are parked near the barn. At least thirty men are also observed milling around the barn and at the entrance of the road leading to the ranch. The area is heavily wooded and a small stream runs nearby. Villa thanks Tool and goes to his office where he calls Ventura and tells him about the information he has just received. He tells him they will wait a few days until the traffickers are well underway with the conversion of the ephedrine into meth. Besides, if the precursors move again, the satellite is still in position to track it. Ventura agrees and states his men are in Colima, Colima, in different hotels and will wait there. Colima, the capital city of Colima, is only nineteen kilometers from the ranch and they can react quickly when the time comes.

Villa then calls the DEA pilots who are assigned to Mexico and work out of the Toluca International Airport. It is about an hour and a half drive from Mexico City. Villa tells them to be on standby with the DEA King Air 350 airplane that is full of sophisticated sensor systems, to include forward looking infrared (FLIR). The FLIR is a valuable tool for the DEA. It consists of a thermographic camera that senses infrared radiation typically emitted from a heat source. Villa knows that the emission from the high energy lights used to dry the processed meth will be easily detected by the FLIR. He briefs the pilots on the ongoing operation and that, he will need them to fly over the ranch in Colima. Villa is in no rush since he knows that converting three tons of ephedrine will be a long and laborious process.

An operational planning meeting is held a few days later between the DEA, Mexican Marines, and federal police at a hangar located on the south end of the Mexico City International Airport. Villa believes in simplicity of plan. He knows that making it too complex with many moving parts will only confuse the participants and can result in the death of his men and those of their Mexican counterparts. In his briefing, Villa tells the federales that their main responsibility will be to establish a perimeter around the ranch to catch the traffickers who try to escape. Once the perimeter has been established, the marines will immediately launch a frontal assault on the ranch using two EC725 Cougar helicopters. The helicopters are equipped with a 12.7mm gun pod and a 7mm rocket pod. They have the capacity to transport twenty-nine soldiers and two pilots. The following morning, they will deploy from Mexico City to a forward operating military base in Zapopan, Jalisco that is one hundred seventy-five kilometers from Cuauhtemoc. It will take less than an hour to reach their target. Villa and Ventura will go in with additional marines in four Bell 212 helicopters belonging to the feds, which have twin Belgium made MAG 7.62mm gun pods and cabin mounted GPMG's (General purpose machine gun). These helicopters will be based at Colima, and will also move into position the following day. Villa ensures that a few of the marines and federales are commingled in order to have critical radio communications between both agencies. Unfortunately, the Mexican federal police and the military don't have compatible communications systems.

Villa reminds everyone that it is important to remember extremely volatile chemicals are used in processing meth and therefore no one should smoke a cigarette within the lab itself. Villa says he will have three DEA agents who have training in clandestine laboratory operations available for the raid. They will have specialized equipment and protective gear to enter the lab and collect valuable evidence. Villa instructs the DEA pilots, in attendance, to overfly the suspected lab site the following evening and determine the level of infrared waves coming from the barn. Villa demands that everyone have raid jackets with visible agency markings so that the various participating agencies will not end up shooting at each other. Everything is set and the deployment of personnel to their designated areas will occur early in the morning.

Villa is startled from a deep sleep when his alarm clock clicks on with a loud, offensive beeping sound. He reaches over and shuts it off. He stares at the ceiling fan for a few minutes and then slowly rolls out of bed. After a long, steamy, hot shower he dresses in brown cargo pants and a black t-shirt. He grabs his Nike athletic bag from his small closet containing his DEA raid jacket, bullet proof vest, and a couple of changes of clothes. He throws the bag into the back seat of his car. It takes him about an hour to arrive at the Mexico City International airport where Ventura is already waiting with several of his men and pilots. After exchanging greetings, they all enter the four helicopters and head west. The sky is overcast and it has started to rain lightly. Villa had always felt a sense of elation in storms and would joke with others that he had probably been born in Transylvania. The uglier the storm, the more comfortable he felt.

Finally, Villa and Ventura accompanied by some of their men arrive in Colima and the helicopters gently land near an isolated hanger, which is filled with several dirty cots, blankets, and tattered pillows. There are several rustic showers lined up in a row sticking out of crumbling, dirty walls. Villa is happy he brought a towel and soap since there are none in the facility. After putting their belongings away under the cots, they settle down to play poker with a ten peso maximum bet. The overall mood is good and everyone is boisterous with fits of howling laughter. Later that evening, Villa goes with one of his men to buy sandwiches, potato chips, and soft drinks for everyone at a nearby restaurant. He pays the bill with his government credit card. It is only right that he covers the food and beverages since Ventura was providing most of the manpower and equipment. The federales had no budget to pay for such expenses and had to literally pay for everything out of their pockets despite their meager salaries.

At about eight that night, Villa receives a call on his HF radio from the DEA pilots. They advise they had just overflown the ranch and the FLIR system picked up an unusually high infrared signature emanating from the barn. Villa thanks them and immediately has Ventura contact the marines to tell them the operation is on at daybreak. The atmosphere immediately becomes somber. Everyone knows there is a possibility some would not return home to their families at the end of the following day. They all go to bed early, but none slept well, mainly catnaps. The adrenaline is already streaming through their bodies preparing them for the potential violent conflict the next day. Very early in the morning, Villa and the others take a quick shower and strap on ballistic vests, weapons, and extra magazines filled with dozens of lethal projectiles. It is a balmy, cloudy morning as they begin to board the helicopters. The federales load all the bags of equipment and check the large machine guns mounted on the sides. The pilots start the rotor blades that whine loudly as they accelerate and gradually the helicopters begin to lift off the tarmac. They head in a northwest direction skirting the ranch slightly where they will rendezvous with the military helicopters so they can assault the ranch simultaneously. The federales on the ground have moved out much earlier and communicate they have already established a perimeter around the ranch. They are concealed and ready to go.

The helicopters circle for less than five minutes before the marine Cougar helicopters approach on the horizon. The noise of the large rotors slicing through the air is deafening, In unison, they all turn westward towards their target. It doesn't take long to see the ranch in the distance. Villa can see lots of vehicles and men walking around with long weapons, undoubtedly AK-47s. The helicopters land about a hundred yards away and everyone quickly jumps out with weapons at the ready. They fan out and the helicopters, once again, rise rapidly into the air. Equipped with heavy machine guns, they will provide critical force protection to the assault teams.

Villa and Ventura sprint towards the ranch as all hell breaks loose. The loud roar of exploding bullets erupts as men seek cover on both sides. Villa can see bullets hitting the ground near him as he dives behind a large boulder. Seconds later, he sees two men with AK-47s running towards him. When they are less than five yards away, he takes quick aim and fires four rounds at them. They fall face first to the ground. Their weapons slide forward in the dry dust. They don't move and are obviously dead. The helicopters open up with their machine guns spewing out hundreds of large projectiles. The barrage of bullets that fill the air find their mark and the carnage is horrific and bloody. The handful of traffickers who survive the initial onslaught throw their weapons on the ground and raise their hands. The soldiers approach them and smash the heavy wooden butts of their long weapons into their backs and arms. The traffickers scream in pain and fall on the ground in total submission. Villa and Ventura proceed to the barn and are surprised to find the largest and most sophisticated laboratory they have ever seen. Closer inspection reveals it is actually a complex of about five separate laboratories. They are structured to facilitate the mass production of meth. On the far end of the barn are the barrels of ephedrine neatly stacked to the rafters. The caustic smell of volatile chemicals permeates the air, despite the large odor extractors that are operating at full capacity.

The traffickers have already processed more than a ton of meth. It is neatly packaged in kilo bricks and wrapped in clear tape. A large amount is still in the process of being dried in large, rectangular steel pans under numerous canopies of powerful heat lamps. As they walk further into the barn, they suddenly find Ochoa, who runs the meth labs for the Blood Alliance Cartel calmly sitting on a chair. He smiles weakly and doesn't put up any resistance. It suddenly strikes Villa that Ochoa prefers a prison cell rather than face the wrath of Atenco. Ochoa knows Atenco will make him suffer a slow torturous death because of the lab seizure. Villa has everyone leave the barn and his agents then enter with their specialized gear to take photos and inventory the entire lab.

The perimeter team captures twelve men and they are brought to the farm house where they will be interrogated. Sixteen traffickers are killed in the operation and only two marines are wounded, but not seriously. The federales use water boarding and, more effectively, the chicharra (cattle prod) to interrogate the traffickers who initially refuse to co-operate.

The long black tubes have two electrodes at the end that blasted painful electrical shocks coursing through their bodies. None are able to withstand more than two shots of it. They all cooperate and declare they work for the Blood Alliance Cartel and their job was to provide security to the lab when it was operational. The chemists who are also captured don't have to be interrogated. They immediately confess that in the past several years, while working for Ochoa and the Blood Alliance Cartel, they have manufactured over two hundred tons of pure meth.

Ventura calls a commercial chemical disposal company to safely dispose of the toxic chemicals. This will prevent them from contaminating the environment or seeping into the water table. His men start to load the remaining barrels of ephedrine and processed meth into the truck, which had transported it from Veracruz.

Upon arriving in Mexico City, the transponders would be removed from the barrels so they could be used again. Ventura now orders his men in Veracruz to immediately arrest the corrupt Customs officials who were complicit in allowing tons of ephedrine to illegally enter the country. Within twenty-four hours they arrest the head of Customs and twenty of his men in Veracruz. They admit to working with the Blood Alliance Cartel and receiving large bribes.

Within hours, Atenco is informed that his main lab has been seized. He goes into a murderous tirade and punches a hole in a million dollar painting by Picasso. He vows revenge against those who were responsible for the operation. He slumps into an oversize sofa and orders one of his men to bring him a bottle of Buchanan scotch. He knew that very few operations happened in Mexico without the involvement and assistance of the DEA. Atenco calls La Sombra and tells him to check with their sources in the federal police and military to find out who was behind the operation. Atenco, sipping his scotch, tells Sombra that the DEA has many informants, but he has even more because DEA's budget is small in comparison to the billions he makes each year. By his third drink, his rage has somewhat subsided. *Eventually, everyone is touched* by *Santa Muerte* (Holy Death), he thought. Fortunately, it is not yet his turn.

CHAPTER
7

Undercover Penetration

Albino Romero is sprawled on a large burnt orange leather couch in one of his safe houses on the outskirts of Juarez, Chihuahua. He watches Mark Potts, a renowned news correspondent from NBC News describe an attack in Europe involving a deadly poison called ricin on his big screen television. Potts went into graphic detail about a Russian KGB defector, Alexander Litvinenko, being injected with ricin by an unknown person using the tip of an umbrella as he walked on a busy street in downtown London. The news story also mentions that the former KGB agent began to exhibit signs of the poison in less than twenty-four hours. Severe nausea, difficulty breathing, heavy sweating, and fever overwhelmed his system. He was hospitalized, but died within three days from the time he was injected with the biological agent. Litvinenko's liver, spleen and eventually both kidney's shut down leading to an agonizing death.

Romero's brain digests the information and begins to go in a hundred different directions as he analyzes the possibilities of using ricin against his expanding list of enemies. It finally dawns on him that he can kill more people with ricin than through conventional weapons. He is still rabidly furious with the Blood Alliance Cartel for the massacre of his men in Chihuahua and envisions killing them all with ricin. Romero begins to smile as more ideas pour into his head. He yells at one of his bodyguards and orders him to fetch Lisa Rochin, one of his most trusted lieutenants and confidantes.

Rochin was a beauty queen who was crowned Miss Chihuahua two years earlier. She beat out a large field of extremely beautiful and talented women. Lisa is an elegant and alluring brunette with sexy almond shaped eyes, but it is her personality that captures the hearts of men. One of Romero's men had dated her for a while and she was immediately smitten with the mafia lifestyle, especially the vast amounts of money involved. She was trained in the use of weapons at rustic firing ranges in mountainous areas and she shows an uncanny ability in the use of handguns and automatic assault rifles. She broke up with her boyfriend after a passionate relationship with Romero who gave her anything she desired. The boyfriend didn't complain, especially since he valued his life. Cartel leaders want the best of everything and have the money to pay for it, including beautiful women. For them, beauty queens are a status symbol of their power and wealth. Women also gravitated to them like moths to a flame.

Romero had dozens of attractive women, but he loved Lisa because she was just as ruthless as any man, if not more. Early in her criminal career, she was ordered to kill a journalist who had become an annoyance to Romero. The reporter constantly wrote inflammatory articles denouncing drug trafficking and actually named Romero as one of the most violent cartel leaders in Mexico. Romero decided to give Lisa the opportunity to prove herself and gave her the contract. It was easy to locate the reporter in the small town where he lived with his wife and four children.

The sun had just begun to come up over the horizon when two black BMW SUV's appeared on the dirt road about a hundred yards from the reporter's house. They stopped and everything was quiet for a few minutes. Lisa, dressed in black, exited one of the vehicles along with three other cartel assassins. They ran quietly to the small adobe house and one of the men swiftly kicked in the flimsy door allowing Lisa to charge into the house. She went into one of the bedrooms and saw several children asleep. They were not her targets and she didn't kill for free. After a quick glance she turned away. She then made her way to the master bedroom as the reporter was jumping out of bed to check on the startling noise in the house. Lisa pointed her Beretta .9mm at his face, which quickly became twisted in terror. He didn't have a chance to speak as she fired three bullets that tore through his skull and the cervical discs in his neck. He was dead as he lifted his arms to protect himself and then crumpled slowly on the wooden floor like a discarded rag doll. His wife screamed in horror.

She rushed to his side and cradled his head on her lap as his blood saturated her nightgown. Lisa stared at her and then walked out the door taking the other assassins with her.

They left the area as quickly as they had come. Lisa felt bad, but with subsequent killings her emotions and compassion become progressively numb to the violence and slaughter. She knew that for her to survive and advance in a male dominated criminal enterprise, she would have to be more ruthless and cunning than most. These traits are admired and respected in the underworld in which Lisa is now a revered figure. Romero liked Lisa because she had bigger "cojones" than most of his men. He said her cojones were so huge, they were bigger than her massive breasts. She was also intelligent and calculating. He can count on her to give him the best possible advice, but more importantly, she is very loyal.

Lisa enters the room wearing tight black satin pants and a revealing red silk blouse that is unbuttoned enough to expose the tops of her voluptuous breasts. She paid thousands of dollars to one of the top plastic surgeons in Mexico for the large bags of silicone. Lisa initially wanted them as normal as possible, but that changed when she decided that bigger was better. Romero's eyes always fixated on them and Lisa would give him a sexy, seductive smile.

She asks, "Albino, me necesitas? Me estaba aburriendo sin nada que hacer." (Albino, do you need me? I was getting bored with nothing to do.)

"Sí, yo estaba viendo un programa interesante en las noticias sobre la ricina. Se puede matar a más cabrones que nuestras ametralladoras. Tengo que conseguir un químico que puede hacer ricina para nosotros. Póngase en contacto con algunos de sus amigos y ver si conocen a alguien. Gracias mi amor." (Yes, I was watching an interesting program on the news about ricin. It can kill more bastards than our machine guns. I have to get a chemist who can make ricin for us. Contact some of your friends and see if they know anyone. Thanks, my love.)

"Albino, he oído hablar de la ricina y es una toxina biológica mortal. Usted tiene que saber que si lo usa, seremos considerados terroristas y los gringos nos va a joder." (Albino, I heard of ricin and it is a deadly biological toxin. You have to know that if you use it, we will be considered terrorists and the Americans will fuck us.)

"Entiendo las consecuencias, pero estamos en una lucha de vida o muerte. Estamos siendo atacados por todos lados, por los gringos y el Cártel de Alianza de Sangre. Sólo temen la violencia y la brutal masacre. Podemos planificar y ponerle la culpa de los ataques ricina a José Atenco. De esta manera podemos expandir nuestras operaciones mientras el gobierno dirigen su atención en él." (I understand the consequences, but we are in a struggle of life and death. We are being attacked from all sides, the Americans as well as the Blood Alliance Cartel. They only fear violence and brutal slaughter. We can come up with a strategy to place the blame of the ricin attacks on Atenco. This way we can expand our operations as the government directs their attention to him.)

Lisa responds, "Está bien, me pondré en contacto con algunas personas que nos puedan ayudar y podemos confiar. Hay muchos químicos, pero necesitamos que también mantendrá la boca cerrada. Sobre la base de lo que han planeado, vamos a necesitar una gran cantidad de ricina. También es posible que tenga que proporcionar un laboratorio donde puede ser fabricado." (Okay, i'll get some people who can help us and we can trust. There are many chemists, but we also need one who can keep his mouth shut. Based on what you have planned, we will need a lot of ricin. You may also have to provide a laboratory where it can be manufactured.)

"Amor, este proyecto es muy importante y necesito que usted resuelva personalmente. Ni se lo digas a nuestros colaboradores más cercanos. Necesitamos que esto permanezca en unas pocas manos. Déjame saber cómo va." (Love, this project is very important and I need for you to handle it personally. Do not even tell our closest collaborators. We need this to stay in a few hands. Let me know how it goes.)

"Vale, Albino. Voy a empezar a trabajar en esto hoy. Tenemos que proceder con mucho cuidado. Hablaremos después." (Okay, Albino. I'll start working on this today. We have to proceed carefully. We will talk later.)

Romero watches as she walks out of the room with her hips swaying slowly back and forth in a seductive manner. He is convinced she can seduce a cadaver without even trying. He doesn't care for too many living things, but he has feelings for her even though he tries hard to suppress them. For him, emotions are a weakness that clouds one's judgment and he can't afford that luxury and remain in control of his billion-dollar drug empire. It had entered his mind that he would marry her, if he lived long enough to retire. He knows the possibility of that is less than a snowball's chance of surviving in hell.

His destiny is either jail or death, not many other options exist for the cartel leader who has to deal with enormous treachery every day. Subordinates will mercilessly destroy him if they see a slight chink in his armor. Even if he survives internal treachery, rivals would be more than happy to murder him without a second thought—it is good business. But like most gamblers, Romero believed he is more cunning and intelligent than his adversaries and therefore can hopefully beat the odds. After all, he has created a multinational organization out of nothing and with little formal education. He also deftly pulls the strings of officials at the highest levels of the government, like so many puppets. They protect him and his organization for money and those that refuse are intimidated into submission.

Lisa starts making calls on her pink cell phone studded with real diamonds. The first person she calls is Rafael, a/k/a *La Serpiente*, not knowing he is a DEA informant. "Rafael, cómo estás? Ha sido bastante tiempo desde que hablamos. Necesito su ayuda en la búsqueda de un químico que podemos confiar. No puedo explicar todo por teléfono así puedes venir a Juárez? Será beneficioso para usted." (Rafael, how are you? It has been quite a while since we talked. I need your help in finding a chemist who we can trust. I cannot explain everything over the phone so can you come to Juarez? It will be beneficial to you.)

Rafael says, "Lisa, me alegro saber de ti después de todo este tiempo. Puedo estar en Juárez mañana por la tarde y nos encontramos en el Hotel Plaza Juárez a las cuatro de la tarde." (Lisa, I'm glad to hear from you after all this time. I can be in Juárez tomorrow afternoon and we can meet at the Hotel Plaza Juarez at four in the afternoon.)

Lisa laughs, "Eso es lo que yo llamo un servicio rápido. Perfecto, te veré mañana." (That's what I call fast service. Perfect, I'll see you tomorrow.)

After ending the conversation, Rafael calls Villa who is working late at the office. As with most calls in Mexico regardless of cell or hardline phones, it is garbled. Fortunately, Villa knew it is Rafael and tells him that he will call him back. "Rafael, dame una buena noticia." (Rafael, give me good news.)

"Escucha, acabo de recibir una llamada de Lisa Rochin, una importante sicaria y confidente de la cabeza del Cártel del Norte, Albino Romero. Se supone que debo de juntar me con ella en Juárez mañana por la tarde. No quería discutir ningún detalle sobre el teléfono. Que quieres que haga?" (Listen, I just got a call from Lisa Rochin, an important assassin and confidant of the head of the Cartel of the North, Albino Romero. I'm supposed to meet her in Juarez tomorrow afternoon. She didn't want to discuss any details over the phone. What do you want me to do?)

Villa tells him, "Viaja a Juárez y reunirse con ella. Yo estaría interesado en ver lo que quiere con usted. No cierres ninguna puerta, independientemente de lo que es, al menos hasta que hable conmigo. En otras palabras, estas abierto a su necesidad. Puede alejarse de la situación más adelante si no es algo que podemos participar, por ejemplo un homicidio." (Travel to Juarez and meet her. I would be interested to see what she wants with you. Do not close any door, regardless of what it is, at least until you talk to me. In other words, be open to her needs. You can always back away from the situation later if is not something we can participate in, such as a homicide.)

"Entiendo. Me voy por la mañana y se reunirá con ella en la tarde. Te llamaré tan pronto que la reunión ha terminado. Tal vez, ella sólo quiere hacer el amor conmigo." (I understand. I will go in the morning and meet with her in the afternoon. I'll call you as soon as the meeting is over. Maybe she just wants to make love to me.)

Villa breaks out in laughter, "Usted debe tener tanta suerte. Sería como si ganar la lotería irlandesa. Usted necesita algunos condones, por si acaso. El mundo no necesita otra serpiente bebé." (You should be so lucky. It would be like winning the Irish lottery. You need some condoms, just in case. The world doesn't need another baby snake.)

The next day, Rafael takes an AeroMexico flight landing at the Juarez International Airport in the early afternoon. He walks through the level one arrival area filled with car rentals, shoe shine stands, and small shops with cheap trinkets for tourists. He is starving, but will wait until he reaches the hotel. Eating airport food is inviting Montezuma's Revenge. He wouldn't eat it even if he was dying of hunger. Outside, vendors are selling whistles, puppets, and black velvet paintings of Elvis in a karate pose. Rafael pushes past them and jumps into a taxicab that has seen better days. The seats are worn and the stuffing is popping out from underneath the cracked artificial leather.

He checks into the 4-star hotel and goes up to his room. It has a king sized bed with a red and yellow comforter. He hangs his clothes in the tiny closet, which also has an old rusty iron and ironing board. A few minutes later, he heads down to the Plaza Grill and sits at a wooden table with swanky red leather chairs. Rafael, like most men who has enemies, sits facing the door. He scans the entire room looking for someone who is out of place and can pose a threat. The young waitress approaches and hands him a menu in a nice dark brown leather folder. At a glance, Rafael orders a bistec ranchero with warm tortillas and a Tecate beer. A short time later, he notices Lisa enter the restaurant in a short black skirt, orange silk blouse, and black pumps. Everything she wears accentuates her feminine attributes. Lisa is accompanied by one of her bodyguards. He looks tough, menacing, and unkempt. He hasn't shaved in days and wears dirty Levi's and a blue western shirt. He glances at Rafael and nods slightly. He takes a table by the door. Lisa smiles and

gives
Rafael a kiss on the cheek smearing her bright red lipstick.

She says, "Rafael, estoy feliz de verte y gracias por venir. Como usted sabes, estamos en una guerra con el Cártel de Alianza de Sangre. Albino quiere matar a tantos de ellos como sea posible. Él ha estado planeando durante varios días y quiere utilizar la ricina en contra de ellos. También quiere usarla contra la DEA, militares, y la policía federal de México. Él me puso a cargo de conseguir un químico confiable para fabricarlo. Sé que tienes un montón de contactos, por eso te he llamado." (Rafael, I'm happy to see you and thank you for coming. As you know, we are at war with the Blood Alliance Cartel. Albino wants to kill as many of them as possible. He has been planning for several days and wants to use ricin against them. He also wants to use it against the DEA, military and federal police in Mexico. He put me in charge of getting a reliable chemist to manufacture it. I know you have a lot of contacts, so that is why I called.)

Rafael, stares at her in disbelief, and says, "Lisa, hablas en serio? Conoce los problemas que podría crear para todos ustedes? Esto podría significar el final de su cártel porque los gringos que vienen después con una venganza." (Lisa, are you serious? Do you know the problems that could be created for all of you? This could mean the end of your cartel because the gringos would come after you with a vengeance.)

Lisa frowns and tells Rafael, "Tienes toda la razón, pero Albino ya a tomado la decisión y él es terco como una mula. Él piensa que él puede hacer que parezca que los ataques fueron realizados por el Cartel de la Alianza de Sangre. De esa manera, los gringos y las fuerzas de seguridad Mexicanas irá tras ellos." (You're absolutely right, but Albino has already made the decision and he is stubborn as a mule. He thinks he can make it appear like the Blood Alliance Cartel carried out the attacks. Therefore, the Americans and Mexican security forces will go after them.)

"Es un movimiento muy arriesgado. Es una estrategia de ganar o perder todo. Posiblemente tengo alguien para ti que puede fabricar ricina, pero voy a ver si puedo ponerme en contacto con él. Ha sido unos años desde que tuve contacto con él. Yo te dejo saber en los próximos días. Por ahora, vamos a tomar unas margaritas y olvidarnos del trabajo."
(It's a very risky move. It is a strategy to win or lose everything. It is possible that I may have someone for you who can manufacture ricin, but i'll see if I can get in touch with him. It has been a few years since I had any contact with him. I'll let you know in the coming days. For now, let's have some margaritas and forget about work.) Lisa grins, and calls the waiter to the table. He rushes over with a white linen cloth on his forearm.

"A sus ordenes." (At your service.)

"Traernos algunos margaritas con el mejor tequila de la casa." (Bring us some margaritas with the best tequila in the house.)

The waiter looks at Lisa and says, "Señorita, estás segura que quieres gastar esa cantidad de dinero? Tenemos la colección 1800 reposado por José Cuervo y es trece mil pesos la botella." (Miss, are you sure you want to spend that kind of money? We have the collection 1800 by Jose Cuervo that is thirteen thousand pesos a bottle.)

Lisa glares at him and yells, "Hijo de puta, qué parecemos que no podemos pagar tu puta tequila? Sólo haz lo que te

pido, y no te preocupes si podemos pagar por su bebida bar-
ata. La próxima vez que usted hace una pregunta tan
estúpida, voy a poner una bala en la rodilla, pendejo."
(Motherfucker, do we look like we can't afford your fucking
tequila? Just do what I ask, and do not worry if we can pay
for your cheap drink. The next time you ask such a stupid
question, I'll put a bullet in your kneecap, fool.)

"Señorita, por favor, perdóname. No era mi intención
ofenderte. Traeré las margaritas de inmediato." (Miss, please
forgive me. I didn't mean to offend you. I'll bring the margaritas immediately.)

After several margaritas, Lisa begins to ramble on everything that comes to her mind. She waves her arms in the air
displaying a large diamond studded bracelet and rings with
ten-carat diamonds.

She whispers, "No menciones esto a nadie, pero Albino
planea utilizar aviones no tripulados comerciales para transportar la ricina a los objetivos previstos. Él ya ha ordenado
veinte de ellos. La belleza es que son tan baratos y fácil de
volar. Y pondrá las ricina en recipientes de vidrio y un
pequeño explosivo por control remoto. De esta manera la
ricina lloverá abajo en la gente que quiere matar." (Don't
mention this to anyone, but Albino plans to use commercial
drones to transport the ricin to the intended targets. He has
already ordered twenty of them. The beauty is that they are
so cheap and easy to fly. He will put the ricin in glass containers and a small remote controlled explosive will expel it
into the air. Thus, ricin will rain down on the people he wants
to kill.)

"Tengo que decir que es ingeniosa. Cómo va a echarle la
culpa al Cártel Alianza de Sangre?" (I have to say it's ingenious. How is he going to blame the Blood Alliance Cartel?)

The margaritas have now completely loosened her lips and her discretion in not disclosing cartel secrets is gone. Besides, she trusts Rafael since he is a professional sicario like her.

"Como he dicho, el objetivo principal va a ser enemigos de Romero. A continuación, las diferentes oficinas de la DEA en todo México van hacer atacados. Él también lo utilizará contra la policía federal mexicana y militar. Él quiere infundir miedo en sus corazones y mentes. Por intimidarlos, serán reacios a atacar nuestro narcotráfico lucrativo." (As I said, the main objective will be Romero's enemies. The different offices of the DEA in Mexico will be targeted. He will also use it against the Mexican military and federal police. He wants to instill fear in their hearts and minds. Through intimidation, they will be reluctant to attack our lucrative drug trade.)

"Sí, usted ha dicho que es el plan, pero cómo va a fijarlo en Atenco y su gente? Yes, you said that's the plan, but how will you pin it on Atenco and his people?)

"Mira, yo te he dicho más de lo que debería tener. Albino va a secuestrar a uno de los subordinados de Atenco y poner sus huellas digitales en uno de los aviones no tripulados y deje que se pueden recuperar. Tras las huellas digitales se colocan con cuidado, el hombre desapareció, nunca para ser visto otra vez." (Look, I told you more than I should have. Albino will kidnap one of Atenco's subordinates and put his fingerprints on one of the drones and allow it to be recovered. After the fingerprints are placed carefully, the man will disappear, never to be seen again.)

Lisa adds, "La belleza es que los drones son hexacopters y el precio es solamente trece mil pesos cada uno." (The beauty is that the drones are hexacopters and the price is only thirteen thousand pesos each.)

The conversation then changes to other topics to include terrorism. Lisa tells Rafael that she had read an article earlier that day about the Islamic State in Iraq and Syria (ISIS).

Lisa says, "ISIS es un montón de maricones. He leído que en 2014 mataron a nueve mil personas en Irak y algunos miles más en Siria. El Cartel del Norte, y otros, en México matamos dieciséis mil en 2013 y más de sesenta mil entre 2006 y 2012. Hemos matado a una persona cada media hora durante los últimos siete años. Operamos en todo México que cuenta con casi dos millones de millas cuadradas e ISIS sólo controla una parte de Irak, que es cuatro veces más pequeño que nuestro país. Ellos sólo han matado a un puñado de periodistas y, desde 2006, nosotros hemos matado al menos a cincuenta y siete. Como usted sabes, operamos en más de sesenta países y tenemos gente trabajando en al menos seis mil ciudades en los Estados Unidos. Nuestra logística es mejor y más expansiva. Hacemos miles de millones de dólares cada año y podemos fácilmente lavarlos a través de bancos internacionales. ISIS son idiotas frente a nosotros." (ISIS is a bunch of faggots. I read that they killed nine thousand people in Iraq and a few thousand more in Syria in 2014. The Cartel of the North, and other criminal groups in Mexico killed sixteen thousand in 2013 and more than sixty thousand between 2006 and 2012. We killed one person every half hour during the last seven years. We operate throughout Mexico that has nearly two million square miles and ISIS only controls a part of Iraq, which is four times smaller than our country. They have only killed a handful of journalists. Since 2006, we killed at least fifty-seven. As you know, we also operate in more than sixty countries and we have people working in at least six thousand cities in the United States. Our logistics are better and more expansive. We make billions of dollars every year and easily launder it through international banks. ISIS terrorists are idiots compared to us.)

Rafael listens intently and says, "Usted sabe, yo nunca había pensado de esa manera, pero tienes razón! Los Americanos están tan centrados en los islamistas radicales que no nos miran como la amenaza más grande. Esto es un gran error por su parte. Una cosa que sí sé es que los cárteles de aquí matan a cerca de seis mil estadounidenses cada año en los EE.UU. en la violencia relacionada con las drogas. Será su caída. No lo crees? (You know, I never thought of it that way, but you're right! Americans are so focused on radical Islamists they do not look at us as the greatest threat. This is a big mistake on their part. One thing I do know is that cartels kill about six thousand Americans in the U.S. each year in drug-related violence. It will be their downfall. Do you not believe it?)

Knowing that she is getting really drunk, Lisa, slurring her words tells Rafael, "Bueno, mejor me voy antes de que ya no puedo caminar. Ha sido bueno verte y voy a esperar a oír de usted, espero que pronto. Ten cuidado." (Well, I better go before I can no longer walk. It was good to see you and I will wait to hear from you, hopefully soon. Be careful.) She stands up from the table and staggers out of the restaurant with her bodyguard trailing behind her.

Rafael, pays the sizable bill and goes back to his room. He calls Villa from his cell phone because he knows that hotel telephones in Mexico are usually monitored by switchboard operators. Most often than not, they form part of the intelligence network of the cartels. Rafael explains the murderous plot by the cartel to use ricin against their enemies, including the DEA. Villa tells Rafael he needs to travel to Mexico City the very next day for a full debriefing. Villa wants Rafael to provide every bit of information Lisa gave him so he can plan his counter strategy.

The next afternoon, Villa meets with Rafael at Sanborn's restaurant about a block away from the U.S. Embassy. Rafael is already at a table when Villa arrives and makes his way through the thick, noisy crowd. Villa addresses him as *La Serpiente*, which makes him smile. He is dressed in black clothes and has oversized sunglasses with small rhinestones on the side. He constantly moves his head back and forth, scanning the vast dining area, checking for potential danger. It is part of situational awareness that is instinctive and practiced by both traffickers and drug agents. It added years to their longevity.

Rafael recounts, in detail, his meeting with Lisa. He says that her boss, Romero, wants to take his revenge against Atenco, the government, and the DEA to a higher level. He tells Villa about Romero's plan to use ricin as a weapon of mass destruction. Ricin is so dangerous that massive collateral damage will also occur and hundreds, maybe thousands will die. Rafael describes the drone that Romero plans on using as the delivery system and Villa immediately identifies it as a Chinese made DJI Spreading Wings S-900 series drone. One had crashed earlier in the year at shopping center in Tijuana carrying about four and a half pounds of meth. It caught the attention of the media in the U.S. who reported that the crash had occurred because the weight of the meth was more than the drone was designed to carry. Villa knew that the assumption was not true. The traffickers knew its specifications and payload capacity fully well. It crashed because the person at the controls screwed up or the drone malfunctioned. Villa knew the drone could fly for eighteen minutes and was easy to transport. It weighed less than three and a half kilograms and the wings made of light carbon fiber could be folded to facilitate transport. It was also very inexpensive as each unit cost one thousand three hundred dollars. Villa thought to himself that the plan was ingenious and extremely deadly.

When Villa tells Rafael that he will pose as the chemist. Rafael gets a concerned look on his face, and in a serious voice asks Villa if he wants to commit suicide. Rafael knows they will eventually figure out that he was the one who informed on them. Villa, however, is an expert in dealing with informants and knew the right things to say to allay their fears. He has been dealing with them for years and knows how to coax them into literally walking into hell and looking forward to the trip. Villa reminds him that he will be taking the same risk and will protect him by getting him legal status in the U.S. for him and his family.

The cartel will not be able to find him. This attracts the attention of Rafael who has always wanted to live in the U.S. He visited Colorado many years ago and fell in love with the area. In less than an hour, Rafael and Villa reach an agreement. Their decision will put both of them in the mouth of a brutal and violent criminal network that never forgets or forgives transgressions against them.

Next, Villa works on a cover story to ensure that he and Rafael are on the same sheet of music. There can be no inconsistencies in their stories and everything they say to Lisa or other members of the cartel have to be the same. Villa spins a story that he and Rafael will use. Villa will use the

fictitious name of Miguel Sanchez. As a cover, he will tell
them that he has a Ph.D in chemistry from New Mexico State
University. Villa concocts a believable story that after graduating, he worked on biological weapons research for the
government until he got tired of the bureaucracy. He made
poor investments and lost most of his fortune so he is des-
perate for money and isn't above doing illegal things, if the
price is right. They labor through all the details and Villa
makes sure Rafael has every last bit of the story down pat.

Villa knows the manufacture of ricin is actually very easy
and doesn't require sophisticated knowledge in chemistry.
The traffickers will not know this and it will be Villa's trump
card. He will make it appear that it is a complicated process
known only by a few specialized chemists. Villa will study
the process, which is on the internet, so he can speak intelli-
gently and be able to answer any questions. For over an hour,
Villa grills Rafael on the cover story until he feels confident
he has it straight. Villa instructs him to wait three days before
he calls Lisa. It would raise suspicions if he came up with a
chemist immediately. Rafael agrees, and in his mind the
sooner he makes the introduction and goes to the U.S. the
better.

Villa is a master at undercover operations because he is a
meticulous planner and develops contingency strategies. He
knows that sloppy operations result in people getting killed
or injured unnecessarily. In the past, he has seen agents lose
their lives because they weren't focused and thought they
could get by flying on the seat of their pants. Working undercover is a deadly business and Villa more than anyone
understands this since death has touched him several times.
There is no room for error, especially when you are dealing

with drug traffickers who are equally cunning and intelligent, but definitely more savage. Villa is of the opinion that no undercover investigation is as dangerous as those involving drug traffickers. Investigations dealing with weapons, money laundering, stolen property, biker gangs, traditional organized crime don't even come close. Absolutely, they are dangerous activities, but certainly not at the same extreme high-risk level.

Villa does exhaustive research on the process for developing ricin. He is surprised that anyone can get the entire process step by step on the internet. With a little research, a terrorist can commit mass killings without having to fire a single shot. He thinks to himself, *Thank God they are not the sharpest knives in the drawer, otherwise the United States and other countries would be in grave danger.*

Villa arranges to have lunch with Ventura at an open air taco stand on a quiet street with large, bushy, fresno blanco trees lining both sides of the narrow street providing a cozy, leafy canopy.

They sit at a cheap white plastic table with matching chairs as one of the workers slices meat from a huge skewer with layers of pork and onions rotating slowly around a fire. There is a whole pineapple impaled on top of the skewer and after slicing meat onto a corn tortilla, the man sporting a green apron chips off a piece of the pineapple with his knife, whirls it up in the air, and catches it behind his back with the tortilla. He does it with the grace of Willie Mays, and never misses once. Villa watches him in awe. Both Villa and Ventura order six tacos al pastor and a couple of ice cold Tecate beers. Villa briefs his close friend on the operation and says he plans to work undercover as a chemist to infiltrate Romero's organization. Ventura smiles and says he can't picture Villa as a nerdy chemist. He reminds Villa that his acting skills will not cost him a bullshit Oscar, but his life if he fails. If they don't believe him, he will die a painful and cruel death. Villa only grins and both dig into their tacos. For a rare moment, they enjoy one of life's small pleasures together.

Four days later, Rafael calls Villa and tells him that he spoke with Lisa and has arranged a meeting in Juarez. It will take place in two days. He casually mentions that she was more than pleased and would pass the information to Romero. Rafael tells Villa that she is very wily and will test him during their meeting to make sure that he is the real thing. Arrangements are then made to meet at the Lucerna Hotel the following evening so they can go over their story one last time.

Later, Villa calls Ventura on his cell and tells him everything is set for the meeting. You can hear the excitement in Ventura's voice. He says Villa can accompany him and several of his men in the Attorney General's Lear jet. Villa declines and says it is best if he flies commercially and not take any chances of someone at the airport seeing him get out of the highly visible and recognizable white and blue jet. Ventura says he will meet Villa the following day in Juarez so they can plan the undercover operation and also have some dinner away from prying eyes.

The next morning, Villa boards a direct AeroMexico flight to Juarez, Chihuahua. The flight is relatively empty except for a lot of screaming kids whose mothers don't even raise an eyebrow as they catapult over the seats and run wildly through the aisles. The flight attendants are having a hard time serving drinks and finally get on the public address system to ask the mothers to control their wild children. The mothers roll their eyes and toss their heads back as though they are offended. One of them yells, "Pedro!" and then goes back to sleep. Villa found it humorous as the frustration levels of the attendants go through the roof and they finally decide to discontinue the beverage and meal service.

When the plane lands in Juarez and slowly taxies to the gate, Villa jumps out of his seat as soon as the bell sounds allowing the passengers to remove their seatbelts. His legs and lower back are stiff from sitting in the uncomfortable and cramped seats. He grabs his carry-on bag, walks out of the terminal, and takes the first available cab. On his ride to the hotel, he observes the ravages of the drug trade on the city, which has converted it into the murder capital of the world for three years in a row. Many of the businesses are boarded up or locked down with heavy metal shutters. The light breeze sweeping through the city kicks up dirt and creates the eerie feeling of a deserted ghost town. Some vendors stand on the practically empty streets hoping to lure American tourists into their stores. Sadly, the tourists are not coming into Juarez, not with the wholesale slaughter that is occurring in the city. Even worse, there is a torrent of kidnappings for ransom taking place in the area. Kidnappings have become a lucrative cottage industry throughout Mexico for common criminals and cartels alike.

Villa finally arrives at the hotel and pays the old taxista four hundred pesos and gives him an additional fifty pesos as a tip. The old man is grateful and says, "Vaya con Dios." Villa hopes the words are not a prophecy of what is to happen in the blood soaked city.

Villa walks through the spacious lobby of the hotel filled with white and yellow cushiony sofas and chairs. The lights are bright and somewhat annoying to the eyes. A bellboy charges towards Villa and grabs his bag. After checking in under the name of Miguel Sanchez, Villa takes the small elevator to the second floor. After entering his room and throwing his bag on the bed, he quickly gives the bellboy a tip who pockets the money and leaves.

After unpacking, he calls Ventura and makes arrangements to meet him in an hour at La Florida restaurant. Villa walks the four blocks to the restaurant and finds Ventura sitting towards the back in a small, wooden table adorned with blue and white, square ceramic tiles. Ventura smiles and graciously pulls out a chair for Villa. He hands him a shot of tequila and they toast to life and their life expectancy, followed by hearty laughter.

They order huachinango (red snapper) smothered in onions and red peppers, Veracruz style. Villa hands Ventura an athletic bag with a mobile tracker and a transponder equipped with powerful magnets to place, if possible, on the undercarriage of Lisa's car. They can then track her movements, at a distance, that will hopefully lead them to Romero. Ventura says he will position surveillance agents in the hotel lobby and in the parking area. After finishing every morsel of the large, delicious fish and having one final tequila for good luck, Villa strides back to the hotel.

A couple of hours later, he receives a call on the hotel phone from Rafael. He says he has just checked in and will come to Villa's room as soon as he unpacks. Fifteen minutes later, there is a loud knock on the door. It is Rafael dressed in black. Even his python boots are black. He is apparently taking his role very seriously.

With a grin on his face he says, "Saludos, Miguel. Cómo estuvo tú viaje? Estaba visitando a unos amigos en el valle de Juárez esta mañana y vi al menos diez cadáveres en el lado de la carretera. Otros cuatro cuerpos decapitados fueron colgados de un puente. Tenían tanto plomo que podrían haber sido utilizados como chatarra." (Greetings, Miguel. How was your trip? I was visiting friends in the Valley of Juárez this morning and saw at least ten bodies on the side of the road. Four other decapitated bodies were hanging from a bridge. They had so much lead in them they could be used as scrap metal.)

Villa responds, "La seguridad de esta ciudad es uno de los peores en el mundo. El Cartel del Norte ha corrompido totalmente y matan a cualquiera que se oponga a ellos. Sólo este año, han matado a seis periodistas que los condenaron en los periódicos. También mataron al Alcalde menos de un día después de que él ganó la elección. También tenemos que tener mucho cuidado ya que todo el departamento de policía de Juárez está en su bolsillo." (The security of this city is one of the worst in the world. The Cartel of the North has totally corrupted it and will kill anyone who opposes them. This year alone, they killed six journalists who condemned them in the newspapers. They also killed the mayor less than a day after he won the election. We also have to be very careful because the entire Juárez police department is in their pocket.)

Rafael says, "Después de nuestra reunión con Lisa, tenemos que tener mucho cuidado de que no nos sigan. Ya le he dicho a Lisa que nos vamos a encontrar con ella mañana. Yo no le dije que ya estaban aquí o en que hotel donde nos quedamos. Ella sólo sabe que la llamaré mañana por la mañana." (After our meeting with Lisa, we must be very careful they don't follow us. I've already told Lisa that we will meet her tomorrow. I didn't tell her we are here or in which hotel we are staying. She only knows that I will call her to-morrow morning.)

"Perfecto! Es important para nosotros mantener la seguridad de lo contrario nos matarán sin pensarlo." (Perfect! It is important for us to maintain security; otherwise they will kill us without thinking about it.)

Villa, after ensuring that the plan is solid, lets Rafael leave in order to get some rest for tomorrow's activities.. He orders a ham sandwich and a glass of red wine for an early dinner and lays in bed watching a Mexican soap opera. It is about a female drug lord who controls a large cartel. It is called, *La Reina de la Mafia*. It goes against the culture of the drug trade, which is definitely dominated by men. It is not an equal opportunity employer. Regardless, Villa finds the program interesting, but rather unrealistic. The actress who plays the primary role doesn't come across as ruthless or violent enough. Villa knows that someone who doesn't possess these traits, especially a woman, will not last a week in the business.

It is the wee hours of the morning when Villa finally goes to sleep. He has a dream of a black vulture standing on a fence post looking down at the dead carcass of a large, black snake. When he wakes up the next day, he vividly remembers the dream and thinks it is rather strange. He is not into Freudian psychology and therefore doesn't try to analyze it.

Villa, uses his cell to call Rafael and asks him to come to his room. He wants to have the call with Lisa tape recorded. About fifteen minutes later, Rafael shows up, wearing the same black clothes, looking like a typical street thug. Villa has to laugh and asks if he slept in his clothes. Rafael lets out a nervous laugh. Villa quickly attaches a small suction cup device on the receiver and turns on the recorder. He hands the phone to Rafael who dials Lisa's number. Villa is surprised the call goes through on the first try. After a short discussion, Rafael hangs up and says Lisa will be over in less than an hour. Villa phones Ventura and gives him a heads up. Ventura has photos of Lisa and already knows what she looks like. Villa begins to psychologically transform himself into his undercover role. He purges any thoughts from his brain about being a federal agent. The adrenaline begins to kick in and he is ready to play the ultimate chess game of life and death.

Forty minutes later, Villa gets a call from Ventura who reports that Lisa has just arrived in the parking lot in a new, black Mercedes Benz. She is accompanied by a large muscular man with short cropped hair. A short time later, there is a soft knock on the door. Villa opens it and allows Lisa and the brutish man into the room. Lisa is dressed in a short red dress with matching shoes. She is dressed to impress Villa. After exchanging greetings, Lisa immediately gets down to business. Villa can tell she is a no nonsense person and doesn't linger on bullshit.

Lisa speaks, "Rafael me dice que usted es un químico capacitado para hacer algún trabajo para nosotros. Estoy seguro de que él ya le ha dicho lo que nos interesa en hacer. Estás dispuesto de hacer este servicio para nosotros?" (Rafael tells me that you are a trained chemist capable of doing some work for us. I'm sure he has already told you what we want to do. Are you willing to do this service for us?)

Villa responds, looking her square in the eyes, "Sí, soy un químico capacitado y especializado en armas biológicas. Tengo una idea de lo que quieren y su uso. Dime lo que usted propone a pagarme y te diré si yo te ayudaré?" (Yes, I am a trained chemist and specialize in biological weapons. I have

an idea of what you want and its use. Tell me what you pro-
pose to pay me and I'll tell you if I will help you?)

Lisa didn't reply to the question and instead asks, "Qué
me puede decir acerca de la ricina y explicame cómo se fab-
rica? También, dime los efectos sobre los seres humanos."
(What can you tell me about ricin and explain how it is
made? Also, tell about the effects on humans.)

"La ricina proviene de la semilla de ricino, que también
se utiliza para hacer aceite de ricino. Se pulsa la semilla para
extraer el aceite, que se utiliza para fines médicos. La ricina,
sin embargo, se extrae a partir del residuo, o torta prensada,
a través de un procedimiento químico que requiere disolventes tales como acetona o hexano. Un buen químico será
capaz de extraer siete miligramos de un gramo de semilla.
Para que tengas una idea mejor, a fin de hacer un kilogramo
de ricina requerirá cerca de mil cuatrocientos treinta kilogramos de semillas de ricino y cinco mil setecientos veinticinco litros de acetona o hexano." (Ricin comes from the
castor bean that is also used to make castor oil. The bean is
pressed to extract the oil, which is used for medical purposes.
Ricin, however, is extracted from the residue, or pressed
cake, through a chemical process, which requires solvents
such as acetone and hexane. A good chemist will be able to
extract seven milligrams from a gram of seed. To give you a
better idea, in order to make a kilogram of ricin will require
about one thousand four hundred thirty kilograms of castor
beans and five thousand seven hundred twenty-liters of acetone or hexane.)

Villa continues, "La ricina es altamente peligroso. Un
adulto promedio necesita sólo menos de dos miligramos de
ricina, ya sea inyectados o inhalados, para morir. Eso es
aproximadamente del tamaño de unos pocos granos de sal de

mesa. La ricina es una proteína tóxica que infecta las células, bloqueando su capacidad de sintetizar su propia proteína. Sin células hacer proteínas, funciones clave en el cuerpo cierran. Cuando se inhala, se desarrollará una tos con sangre y los pulmones se llenan de líquido y dejas de respirar." (Ricin is highly dangerous. An average adult needs only less than two milligrams of ricin, either injected or inhaled to die. That's about the size of a few grains of table salt. Ricin is a toxic protein that infects cells, blocking their ability to synthesize their own protein. Without the cells making proteins the key functions in the body shut down. When inhaled, the person will develop a bloody cough and the lungs fill with fluid and the person is likely to stop breathing.)

Lisa listens intently, but Villa knows she doesn't understand the complex explanation about ricin. But she certainly is aware that it is extremely deadly. She glances at the man sitting in the corner as though wanting a sign that he understands what Villa is saying. He only nods his head and his facial expression is a frozen scowl. He is incapable of smiling.

Lisa asks, "Dónde vas a obtener una gran cantidad de semillas de ricino porque nos gustaría que usted haga cinco kilogramos de ricina, para empezar? Tiene planes para su fabricación en los Estados Unidos o en México?" (Where will you get such a large quantity of castor beans because we would like you to make five kilograms of ricin, to begin with? Do you plan to manufacture it in the United States or Mexico?)

"Puedo pedir el ricino de China. Hay una empresa llamada Hebei Trading donde puedo comprar toneladas de las semillas. El costo es novecientos sesenta y cinco dólares por tonelada. Si quieres cinco kilos de ricina en un principio, voy a pedir un poco más de siete toneladas. Voy a fabricarlo aquí en México, ya que será fácil introducir las semillas en el país con la ayuda de Rafael. El también me va conseguir un lugar aislado donde puedo hacer la ricina." (I can get the castor beans in China. There is a company called Hebei Trading where I can buy tons of the beans. The cost is about nine hundred sixty-five U.S. dollars per ton. If you want five kilos of ricin initially, I will ask for a little more than seven tons. I'm going to manufacture it here in Mexico, because it will be easier to introduce the beans into this country with the help of Rafael. He can also get me an isolated spot where I can make the ricin.)

"Muy bien. Cuál es el precio con el fin de trabajar para nosotros en este asunto?" (Very good. What is your price in order to work for us on this matter?)

Villa replies, "Este es un asunto muy delicado y muy peligroso. Si me descubrí, voy a hacer considerado un terrorista y enviado a prisión por el resto de mi vida. La única razón por la que voy a hacer esto es porque necesito el dinero. Quiero una combinación de dinero y cocaína. Quiero cien mil dollares en efectivo y cincuenta kilos de cocaína. Quiero la mitad de cada uno de ellos por adelantado y la otra mitad cuando se acaba el trabajo. Esto no es negociable. Si usted piensa que esto es demasiado, entonces me iré. Es tu decisión." (This is a very delicate and very dangerous business. If I am discovered, I will be labeled a terrorist and sent to prison for the rest of my life. The only reason I'm doing this is because I need the money. I want a combination of money and cocaine. I want one hundred thousand dollars in cash and fifty kilos of cocaine. I want half of each in advance and the other half when the job is finished. This is not negotiable. If you think this is too much, then I'll leave. It is your decision.)

"Entiendo. No tengo ningún problema con su proposición. En realidad, pensé que ibas a pedir más. Puedo tener la mitad del dinero y de la cocaína en unas pocas horas. Qué tan rápido puede usted comenzar a hacer la ricina?" (I understand. I have no problem with your proposal. Actually, I thought you were going to ask for more. I can have half the money and cocaine in a few hours. How fast can you start making the ricin?)

"Bueno, entonces tenemos un acuerdo. Yo soy un hombre de negocios, no un ladrón. Sé que podría haber pedido más, pero quiero desarrollar una relación comercial de largo con usted. Las semillas de ricino se llevará unos veinte días en llegar a México. Puedo conseguir fácilmente el equipo de disolventes y de laboratorio aquí en México. Tomará varias semanas para procesar los cinco kilogramos de ricino puro." (Well, then we have an agreement. I am a businessman, not a thief. I know I could have asked for more, but I want to develop a long business relationship with you. The castor beans will take about twenty days to reach Mexico. I can easily get equipment and laboratory solvents here in Mexico. It will take several weeks to process five kilograms.)

Lisa, in a quiet voice, says, "Bueno. Tenemos un trato. Voy a conseguir el dinero y la cocaína muy pronto. Estás de suerte porque acabamos de recibir un envío reciente y lo tenemos almacenado cerca. Voy a volver pronto y podamos seguir adelante." (Good. We have a deal. I'll get the money and cocaine quickly. You're in luck because we just got a recent shipment and have it stored nearby. I will return soon and we can move forward.)

Lisa and Villa shake hands. Villa can't help notice all the diamonds that cover all of her fingers and wrists. There are so many that their brilliance illuminates the entire room, certainly a few hundred thousand dollars worth that were paid in full by blood money. Lisa slowly rises to her feet and nods at the man who is obviously her bodyguard. He shows no emotion. He quietly follows her out of the room.

Rafael, breathes a sigh of relief, and says, "Usted fue cojonudo! Yo no sabía que usted sabía mucho acerca de la ricina. Usted, literalmente, me había convencido de que usted era un químico real. Lisa se tragó todo lo que le dijiste. Solo tengo una pregunta. Porqué le pide un poco de cocaína? (You were fucking great! I didn't know that you knew so much about ricin. You, literally, had me convinced you were an actual chemist. Lisa swallowed everything you said. I have only one question. Why did you ask for some cocaine?)

"Quiero la cocaína para que podamos hacer un caso fuerte de drogas y tal vez podamos identificar su almacén de droga." (I want the cocaine so that we can make a strong drug case against them and maybe we can also identify their drug warehouse.)

Villa calls Ventura and tells him Lisa is on her way down. Ventura mentions they saw her when she arrived earlier and one of his men parked next to her car as though he was a guest of the hotel. As he got down from his car, he pretended to drop something and quickly placed the device under Lisa's Mercedes Benz. They then moved out of the parking lot and are now getting a strong signal on the mobile tracker that is monitoring the transponder. Suddenly, Ventura mentions that Lisa is walking out the front door of the hotel with her bodyguard whom he describes as a Neanderthal. Villa tells him to let the tracker do its job and they can follow Lisa at a safe distance. Villa knows she will be checking for a tail and the entire operation can be jeopardized if she thinks she is being followed. Ventura tells Villa not to worry; he has his best and most trusted men working with him.

Lisa calls Romero as she is driving out of the hotel parking lot. "Albino, acabo de conocer el químico y él sabe lo que está hablando. Estoy convencida de que él es la cosa real, ya que respondió a todas mis preguntas. Él está pidiendo cien mil dólares y cincuenta kilos de cocaína con la mitad delantera. Le dije que no sería un problema. Estoy en camino al almacén principal para conseguirlo." (Albino, I just met with the chemist and he knows what he is talking about. I am convinced that he is the real thing because he answered all my questions. He is asking for one hundred thousand dollars and fifty kilos of cocaine with half up front. I said it would not be a problem. I'm on my way to the main warehouse to get it.)

"Esa es una muy buena oferta. Esa cantidad para nosotros no es nada. Cuánto tiempo va tomará para producir la ricina? Asegúrese de que no se siguen." (That's a very good deal. That amount for us is nothing. How long will it take him to produce the ricin? Make sure you are not followed.)

"Él tendrá que pedir varias toneladas de semillas de ricino procedentes de China y tardará unos veinte días para llegar en México. Quiere hacer la ricina en nuestro país y me imagino alrededor de un mes para procesar una vez que llegue. Me aseguraré que nadie me sigue. Hablaremos después." (He will have to order several tons of castor beans from China that will take about twenty days to arrive in Mexico. He wants to make the ricin in our country and I guess it will take about a month to process once it arrives. I'll make sure no one follows me. We will talk later.)

Lisa begins to take evasive measures by making quick turns, going into dead end streets, and making U-turns on busy streets. She is unaware that she is being followed from a mile away and her tactics don't matter. The transponder underneath her car and the monitor in Ventura's car are in sync and she won't be able to shake the moving surveillance. Of course, there is always the chance of an electronic malfunction, but the probability is slim since it is state-of-the-art equipment and brand new. Ventura is moving slow and keeping his men even further behind him. He knows that many of his agents have limited operational capabilities, but he continually trains and mentors them.

Through Villa, he has attended numerous training courses at the DEA academy in Quantico. As a result, Ventura has become a first rate investigator and is extremely capable as a field commander. He is proud that he can be a leader to his men as Villa is to him.

Ventura contacts Villa on his cell to advise him of Lisa's movements and that she is definitely checking for a tail. She is now parked at a convenience store and standing in front checking for suspicious activity. As he mentions this, he lets Villa know that she is back in her car and is on the move again. Villa tells him not to worry, she will eventually have to make the pickup and lead them to the stash location. They hung up and Villa goes with Rafael down to the hotel restaurant to get something to eat. Both are famished. They each order a porterhouse steak with a baked potato. As they eat and kill time, Villa asks Rafael how he had got the nickname of "Serpiente (snake)."

Rafael smiles at the question and says, "Bueno, cuando yo era un asesino a sueldo se dice que nadie me vio antes de que yo los maté. Llamó la atención que yo era tan rápido como una serpiente de cascabel. Por lo que un amigo mío, también es un asesino, me nombró la serpiente y se quedó."

(Well, when I was a hired assassin, it is said that no one saw me before I ended their lives. They noticed that I was as fast and lethal as a rattlesnake. So a friend of mine, also an assassin, named me the snake and it stuck.)

As they were about to finish eating, Ventura calls and says that Lisa's car is parked at a large house on the outskirts of Juarez. It is a two-story brick colonial house that has a large lawn in front. There are two other cars at the house and he has been able to get the license numbers. Next to the house is a rundown home, which appears to be abandoned. Tall, dry weeds and several Chinese elms surround it. Villa tells him to stay on her in case she goes to another location or meets with someone. Ventura laughs. He knows what Villa would say before he says it. Great minds think alike, he thought.

Over an hour goes by and finally Ventura calls and says that Lisa is on the road and headed in the direction of the hotel. This time she doesn't appear to check if anyone is following. Later, Ventura calls again and reports that Lisa has pulled into the hotel parking lot and she and her bodyguard have taken a couple of suitcases out of the trunk. They are walking slowly into the hotel. As expected, there is a loud knock on the door and Villa opens the door. Lisa enters with the elegance of a queen, followed by her expressionless thug. They unceremoniously throw the suitcases on the bed and unzip them.

Lisa says, "Este es el pago inicial de cocaína y dinero. Voy a necesitar que me mantenga al tanto de su progreso, una vez que llegan las semillas de ricino. Toda la comunicación será a través de Rafael. Por cierto, si algo va mal, tanto usted como Rafael tendrá que pagar con sus vidas. No toleramos la incompetencia o la traición. Ha quedado claro.

Usted pidio la cocaína, qué vas a hacer con élla?" (This is the initial payment of cocaine and money. You need to keep me informed of your progress once the castor seeds arrive. All communication will be through Rafael. By the way, if something goes wrong, you and Rafael will pay with your lives. We do not tolerate incompetence or betrayal. Is that clear? You asked for cocaine, what are you going to do with it?"

"Voy a vender la cocaína en los EE.UU. Tengo un primo que vende drogas y él va tomar cargo de la distribucion. Esto significa una gran cantidad de dinero para mí." (I will sell the cocaine in the U.S. I have a cousin who sells drugs and he will take charge of the distribution. This means a lot of money for me.)

"Esta bien. Solo se cuidadoso. No queremos que nuestros planes con la ricina en ruinas. Vamos a permanecer en contacto. Nos vemos más tarde." (It's okay. Just be careful. We do not want our plans with ricin in ruins. Let's keep in touch. See you later.)

Lisa turns and leaves with her bodyguard in tow. Villa calls Ventura and gives him a heads up. He tells Ventura that they will meet later to discuss the next steps of the operation.

CHAPTER 8

The Capture

After Lisa leaves, Villa goes to meet with Ventura at the Hotel Conquistador Inn to discuss strategy on the ongoing operation. He uses some of Ventura's men to conduct counter-surveillance to make sure that he isn't being followed. As Villa travels in a small, brown Ford taxi, Ventura's men follow discretely behind and scan cars to make certain that Villa was not being tailed. If another car makes every turn and follows every street traveled by Villa, Ventura's men will suspect a tail and investigate. Villa also has the cab driver take a random route under the pretense of doing a little bit of sightseeing. The driver, an old toothless man with disheveled gray hair, wasn't suspicious since his only concern is making more money. Eventually, Villa receives a text message saying, *NO HAY PROBLEMA* meaning that the coast is clear.

Forty-five minutes later, Villa arrives at the four-story hotel, which has a very unusual color combination. The upper floors of the outer walls are painted a light brown, but the ground level is a bright red. To the right of the entrance and attached to the hotel is the restaurant Mestizo, which is wrapped in a white wrought iron fence that seems totally out of place. Villa pays the cab driver and gives him a nice tip, which causes him to grin broadly. He grabs the money, like it might get away, and drives off with the car's engine rattling loudly from poor quality gasoline. Villa goes through the immaculate lobby garnished with small palm trees in colorful, hand painted pots. He takes the small elevator adorned with full-length mirrors for guests who take great pleasure in admiring their reflections as they move between floors.

Finding Room 401, Villa knocks on the door and is quickly let in by Ventura who is accompanied by three of his men. Ventura gives Villa an abrazo and hands him a shot glass of tequila. Villa downs it and they all sit around a small, wooden coffee table. A bottle of Don Julio is in the middle of the table with slices of fresh lime in a crystal bowl. Ventura jokingly tells Villa he can be a big star in Hollywood and win a bunch of Oscars. He adds that Villa should be included in the walk of fame at the Grauman's Chinese Theatre. Hell, he says, none of Hollywood's actors have ever risked their lives on their ability to create reality for an audience as you have so many times. They all laugh and have another shot then bite into the bitter, juicy lime, which Villa finds very refreshing.

Villa hands two dark vinyl mesh bags containing the money and the cocaine to Ventura who will keep them as evidence until needed. After Ventura looks into them, he hands the bags to one of his men for safekeeping. Villa also gives him a small piece of paper with Lisa's telephone number, which Rafael gave him.

Villa suggests, "We need to put a tap on the phone and use a pen register to see what numbers she is calling and the also the numbers that are calling her. She is tight with Romero and hopefully, she will lead us right to him."

Ventura replies they will be on it by the following day. He also mentions that he will be leaving several of his men in Juarez, but they will stay in El Paso at night for security reasons.

Villa comments that the location where Lisa went to pickup the money and drugs can't be raided immediately since it will compromise Rafael and the operation. After talking about several options, both men agree on a viable strategy. They will wait several days, keeping the stash house under surveillance, and then one night will start a fire by throwing gasoline on the weeds in the adjacent abandoned house. They don't want to endanger firefighters needlessly so they will make it appear that a routine marine patrol in the area spots the fire and responds. Military units, due to the brutal and massive violence, saturate the city so it will not appear unusual. The marines will go to the stash house and make the occupants evacuate the house for obvious safety reasons. Pretending to search the house to make sure everyone is out will give them the opportunity to search for drugs and money. Ventura is happy with the plan and decides to stay in Juarez so nothing is left to chance. He will also coordinate the operation with the marines. As nightfall approaches,

Villa goes to the airport to catch a flight back to Mexico City. He sits alone at a small restaurant and orders a hamburger, but the bread is stale and the meat tastes worse than dog food. He throws it into a garbage can and goes looking for a decent meal. He finds a clean outdoor restaurant and has four large tacos with hot sauce from a bottle and a cold diet coke. They hit the spot and he feels much better.

It is a dreary, rainy day in the mountains near the municipality of Badiraguato, Sinaloa. Drug lord Atenco sits in a spacious living room on an oversized couch decorated with blue, yellow, and maroon pillows. La Sombra is facing him sitting on a yellow, leather love seat. He feels anxious when he sits on couches that seem to swallow him. Closeness to anything, including couches makes him feel suffocated and weak. He finally stands up from the couch and finds a wooden chair, settles in and his anxiety immediately goes away.

Atenco takes a sip of Presidente brandy and says, "He estado en contacto con Carlos Mejía, jefe del Frente 72 de las FARC, en Colombia. Estamos finalizando una operación de diez toneladas de cocaína. Carlos debe estar listo para enviar la cocaína en unos tres días. Tenemos que preparar todo de nuestra parte para asegurarse de que nada va mal." (I have been in contact with Carlos Mejia, head of the 72nd Front of the Armed Revolutionary Forces of Colombia (FARC). We are finalizing an operation of ten tons of cocaine. Carlos should be ready to ship the cocaine in three days. We have to prepare everything on our end to make sure nothing goes wrong.)

"Si jefe. Vamos a estar listos y hemos tomado las precauciones con el gobernador para asegurar que la policía va a estar lejos de nosotros. Tuvimos que pagar algo de dinero, pero vale la pena." (Yes, Boss. We will be ready and have taken precautions with the governor to ensure that the police will be far away from us. We had to pay some money, but it is worth it.)

La Sombra met Mejia when he visited Atenco in Mexico several months earlier. Mejia is short, squat, with curly hair mopped under a disgusting, filthy beret sitting lopsided on his head. He didn't look like a typical guerilla, but more like a French accountant who is a maricon. Mejia is being groomed to become a member of the FARC's Secretariat, consisting of seven top leaders, which is the governing body of the eighteen thousand armed combatants fighting to overthrow the elected government of Colombia. The FARC started its struggle in 1964, initially fighting for the rights of poor farmers. Then slowly, their ideology shifted to protecting clandestine laboratories and airstrips belonging to drug trafficking organizations.

Eventually, they became intoxicated with the wealth from drug trafficking and whatever ideological motives they had were chucked into the toilet. They transformed themselves into the biggest drug distribution organization in Colombia.

La Sombra doesn't trust Mejia, but knows he is an important source of cocaine to the cartel. La Sombra is is rapidly becoming familiar with the routes, methods of transportation, conveyances, sources of supply, money laundering, and the corrupt politicians that Atenco has in his pocket like so many centavos (pennies). He is enjoying his relationship with Atenco and works hard to always explore better methods and routes to smuggle drugs and expand distribution in the U.S. He also wants to expand into other countries, which will increase profits. La Sombra knows that together with his friend, Atenco, they will create the most powerful criminal network in the world. Everyone, including governments around the globe, will fear it. They will become a shadow government that will pull the strings of legitimate governments. Those who oppose them will be dismembered like animals in a butcher shop. La Sombra knows that the fear of a painful, gruesome death is crippling and causes men to do things they would never dream of doing in a million years. It is fear that grips the most hardened men until it breaks them psychologically. They just can't get it out of their minds. It is a huge tool in the arsenal of drug cartels. La Sombra had a PhD in the application of fear and intimidation.

La Sombra, several months earlier, had convinced Atenco to purchase two used Boeing 727 commercial jets. They were able to get a good deal and paid slightly less than a million dollars for each one. La Sombra had one of the cartel attorneys create a fictitious transport company called Aero Transportes Mexico. The attorney was conveniently a notary public so he notarized all of the legal paperwork. They also rented a small office in Guadalajara and paid a naïve young girl to just answer the telephone. In the event someone wants legitimate transportation services, she is instructed to tell them that they are booked up for several months.

La Sombra looked at several aircraft, which were capable of transporting quite a few tons of cocaine at a time. He finally chose the 727 because of its ability to land on shorter runways due to its wing design and no wing mounted engines. The planes have a cruising speed of five hundred and seventy miles per hour and a top speed of six hundred and thirty-two miles per hour. This means that the only thing that can intercept it is a military jet fighter. La Sombra also likes the fact that they have a range of three thousand one hundred and ten miles and flew at a ceiling of thirty-six thousand feet. He calculated the distance from Colombia to Sinaloa as two thousand six hundred miles, well within its range. The planes are stored in hangars at the Guadalajara International Airport with hundreds of other commercial aircraft and no one gives them a second glance.

La Sombra hires a small army of campesinos (peasant farmers) to carve out a clandestine, dirt airstrip on a flat piece of land in an isolated area north of Culiacan. It takes weeks to build using only picks, shovels, and old wheelbarrows. To clear the brush, they use sharp machetes. The strip is accessible by vehicle through a rough mountain trail. La Sombra makes sure the campesinos are well fed. They built a small kitchen made of ply board. Propane gas is used to cook the meals in large ten-gallon pots. The cooks are three older women who live nearby. They can turn potatoes, celery, and onions into a gourmet meal. The women use flat skillets to crank out flour tortillas, which they keep warm under small towels. When the airstrip is not in use, it is covered with foliage placed on large wooden platforms with wheels that are rolled onto the strip using large ropes. This prevents anyone from discovering it from the air. The campesinos are also paid to provide security to the airstrip and to make sure that it is not under surveillance before using it to bring in a load of cocaine.

Two days before the operation, La Sombra begins to coordinate with the FARC using an encrypted Motorola radio, which has VHF, UHF, and HF frequencies. They have code words, which only they know such as:

Cocaine—Amigo (Friend)
Aircraft—Novia (Girlfriend)
Money—Libros (Books)

Tons—Semana (Week) The number of weeks correlated to the tons involved.

They also have a list of radio frequencies that are changed on each operation. La Sombra contacts the FARC and asks if the "amigo" is ready for his trip? He also said that they would expect him in ten weeks and that his "novia" will go pick him up. In code, he asks if the cocaine is ready and that they want ten tons, which their aircraft will transport. He also mentions that they will send a hundred books, meaning that an initial down payment of a hundred million dollars will be sent to the FARC. Everything is set and now the complex logistics and coordination will be critical to the operation. One of their 727's is fueled and two retired AeroMexico pilots who now work for the cartel are told to get ready to travel to Colombia. Each pilot usually makes two hundred thousand dollars per trip. They are indispensable and can be trusted. They also have the skills to land and take off from unimproved landing strips.

La Sombra also alerts a hundred gunmen to get ready to provide armed security to the airstrip when the aircraft lands with the tons of cocaine. All of them will be carrying AK-47 assault rifles and handguns. Some of them will also have rocket propelled grenade launchers. For Mexican security forces to be able to overcome a force this size will require at least an equal number or larger of police or military elements. A smaller unit will result in a bloody massacre. It is highly unlikely the police or military will be able to deploy that number of personnel, especially in such a remote area. La Sombra also has another distinct advantage, Mexico's security forces are highly disorganized and they don't delegate authority. In other words, if the commanders or supervisors of the various security forces are not available, their subordinates are not allowed to react. This usually prohibits a quick reaction to tactical operations. Most operations against drug traffickers are tactical and fast breaking.

It is a bright, sunny morning, when La Sombra has four of his men arrive at the Guadalajara airport with a truckload of boxes labeled as containing air conditioning units. They are stuffed with U.S. dollars in denominations ranging from ten to hundred dollar bills. They approach a security checkpoint and a young guard wearing a blue polyester uniform is in a heated argument with his girlfriend on the telephone and impatiently waves them through. It takes less than fifteen minutes to load the aircraft. The pilots have already filed a flight plan to Bogota and they begin to go through their meticulous written checklist prior to take off, which includes:

- o Auxiliary fuel pump — Off
- o Flight controls — Free and correct
- o Instruments and radios — Checked and set
- o Landing gear position lights — Checked
- o Altimeter — Set
- o Directional gyro — Set
- o Fuel gauges — Checked
- o Trim — Set
- o Engines — Exercise
- o Magnetos — Checked
- o Engine idle — Checked
- o Flaps — As required
- o Seat belts/shoulder harnesses — Fastened
- o Parking brake — Off
- o Doors and windows — Locked
- o Mixture — Full rich unless above 3,000 feet
- o Lights — Landing, taxi, strobes on

o   Camera — Transponder on

o   Action — Engine instruments checked

The pilots meticulously go step by step through the long checklist. Too often, they have seen other pilots ignore standard procedures and most of them are now six feet below the surface of the earth. They also know that the cocaine they are transporting is worth hundreds of millions of dollars, if not billions. Their bosses will react most violently if they crash the plane because of negligence. It will mean that one generation, maybe two, of their family tree will be summarily erased from the planet. The money they are paid was phenomenal, but they are under no illusions; they can potentially land in prison, die in a crash, or worse incur the wrath of their masters.

The pilots contact the control tower and request permission to take off. The control tower instructs them to wait since American flight 234 from Dallas is on its landing pattern. Five minutes later, the control tower clears them for takeoff. The plane slowly makes its turn onto the runway. The pilots push the throttles forward and the plane begins to quickly accelerate. As the plane gains speed, the wings produce more lift and begin to support more of the plane's weight. The pilots tip it upwards slightly, dramatically increasing the lift. It ascends effortlessly into the sky like a massive bird of prey. The plane accelerates even more since the wheels are no longer rolling on the ground to slow it down. Once the wheels are retracted, it flies faster and climbs higher. When the plane reaches cruising altitude, the pilots lean back in their black leather chairs and settle in for the trip southward. They have already set the coordinates for their destination, decimal degrees, Latitude 0.4525000/Longitude 76.9191700. They are heading to a

FARC stronghold near the Valle de Guamuez in the department (state) of Putomayo, Colombia, near the border with Ecuador. The elevation of the landing strip located there is three hundred and thirty-six meters above sea level. One of the pilots checks and determines that it is seventy-five degrees Fahrenheit and the wind is west at two miles per hour at their destination. Their patron saint, Jesus Malverde, is with them making sure all goes well. The pilots remind themselves to take flowers to Malverde's shrine upon their return to Sinaloa. After several hours, the 727 starts its descent towards the landing strip and communication is established with FARC rebels on the ground. The crackle of their radio transmission has loud static, but is understandable.

"Novia, podemos oír sus motores. Estamos listos para usted y todo está seguro," says the FARC commander on the field. (Girlfriend, we can hear your engines. We're ready for you and everything is safe.)

"Novia aqui, empezamos nuestro descenso y debemos aterrizar en unos veinte minutos. Tienen el combustible para el viaje de regreso? Queremos pasar el menor tiempo en la pista de aterrizaje." (Girlfriend here, we started our descent and should land in about twenty minutes. Do you have fuel for the return trip? We want to spend as little time as possible on the runway.)

The rebel commander seems annoyed, "Cree que nos olvidaríamos el puto combustible? Por supuesto, tenemos combustible. Vete al otro extremo de la pista de aterrizaje y lo llenamos con conbustible y cargamos el amigo allí también. La pista de aterrizaje está en perfecto estado. También tenemos comida y agua para su regreso. Buena suerte." (Do you think we would forget the fucking fuel? Of course, we have fuel. Go to the end of the runway and we will refuel and load the cocaine there. The runway is in perfect condition. We also have food and water for your return. Good luck.)

The pilots begin to perform their landing checklist to make sure that all critical items such as fuel flow, landing gear down, and lower flaps, are not forgotten. They stabilize the airspeed and rate of descent, aligning the plane with the runway. The plane drops slowly and touches down perfectly. It is a bumpy landing, however, since the strip is not even and the tires go over rocks and potholes. It eventually slows and rolls to the end of the runway where several trucks are parked. The pilots look out the window and see what appear to be at least a hundred rebels dressed in green camouflage fatigues. Wrapped around their left arms are yellow, red, and blue armbands. They are the colors of the Colombian flag. The recognizable acronym FARC is also on the bands.

After shutting down the engines, the pilots get off the aircraft and are immediately approached by the rebel commander who is in his late forties. He is Mejia'a right hand man. He has a strong, yet slender build. He wears a beret and has a long, stringy beard, obviously trying to emulate Che Guevara. He carries an AK-47 that has seen better days and is surrounded by eight other rebels who are his personal praetorian guard.

"Bienvenidos! Nos ocuparemos de todo. Vamos a descargar el dinero y cargar la cocaína lo más rápido posible. Al mismo tiempo, vamos a llenar el avión con combustible, mientras que ustedes tengan algunos refrescos. No hay que preocuparse, este es nuestro territorio y las fuerzas gubernamentales tienen miedo de venir aquí," he said. (Welcome! We'll take care of everything. We will offload the money and load the cocaine as quickly as possible. At the same time, we will refuel the plane while you have some refreshments. Not to worry, this is our territory and government forces are afraid to come here.)

The pilots walk over to a group of female FARC members who hand them hard bread, dried, spicy slices of beef or at least something that tastes like beef. They are too afraid to ask what it is. The pilot's notice some of the females are barely twelve to fourteen-year-old girls and carry handguns and assault rifles. In conversation with one who is about thirty years old, the pilots learn that women make up about thirty percent of the FARC. One attractive female says she is from Barranquilla. She explains the females are expected to carry out the same duties as their male counterparts. They fight alongside the men in combat against government troops. They also build and plant homemade land mines. At times, they dress in civilian clothes and gather intelligence, reporting on the movements of the Colombian army. When needed they work as nurses and perform first aid. But worse, they recruit children into the rebel ranks, many of whom don't last more than a few weeks before they are killed. This bothers the pilots because both have children. They know they are criminals, but have a sense of decency and concern when it comes to innocent kids.

As the loading of the cocaine continues, one of the pilots says he needs to urinate and walks into a nearby wooded area. A few minutes later, the pulsating beat of helicopter rotors can be heard rapidly approaching. Suddenly, a few feet above the treetops, five OH-58 helicopters close in on the clandestine airstrip.

The FARC commander yells, "Es la policía de mierda! Abren fuego y maten a los bastardos! Movense rápidamente, compañeros!" (It's the fucking police! Open fire and kill the bastards! Move rapidly, comrades!)

The loud and overlapping screams of FARC soldiers is quickly drowned out by the piercing sounds of automatic weapons fire from the rebels. The helicopters make a quick pass to get their bearings and do a series of sharp turns to get a better line of fire. The mounted GAU-19A's with six-barrel configurations are modified to fire eight thousand rounds per minute. In less than half a second they reach their maximum firing rate. They spit fire and lead covering just about every square inch of the area.

The bullets rapidly penetrate the aircraft, trucks, and pierce human bodies on the strip like an ice pick through soft butter. The plane disintegrates in minutes and white powder floats through the air like a major snowstorm. The bloody carnage is over quickly and reddish shreds of human flesh gruesomely cover the vegetation, rocks, and ground. Three of the helicopters land close by, while the other two provide protection from above. It is not needed. The area is devoid of all human life, except one.

The pilot who went into the woods comes out from hiding and cautiously approaches the police officers on the field. When he gets sight of the massacre, he has a fit of projectile vomiting. He thinks *this has got to be what hell looks like*. His nausea returns over and over again, but he has nothing left in his stomach to vomit.

General Leonardo Gallego, dressed in a green jungle uniform, jumps from one of the helicopters and makes his way to the pilot. The General has chiseled features and a medium build with dark hair parted to one side. He has a formidable command presence. He is known as the *Lion of Colombia* for his courage and valiant struggle against some of the most powerful drug lords in the world who are virtual killing machines. He has led some of the more daring operations in the history of Colombia resulting in the killing or imprisonment of numerous cartel heads. All of his men will loyally follow him to the Circle of Hell in *Dante's Inferno* and back. He always leads from the front and never from the rear.

The General tells the pilot, "Miguel Villa envía sus saludos. En pocos minutos, estaré en contacto con él por radio para hacerle saber que la operación fue un éxito. La cocaína no se va al norte y hemos acabado con toda una columna de la FARC. La mayor parte del dinero es rescatable. Usted va a venir con nosotros y estaremos enviandolo mañana en un vuelo comercial a Miami, Florida. Miguel quiere que sepas que ya ha enviado a su familia a los EE.UU. y está coordinando con la inmigración para que pueda vivir allí." (Miguel Villa sends his greetings. In a few minutes, I'll be in radio contact with him to let him know that the operation is a success. The cocaine is not going north and we wiped out an entire column of the FARC. Most of the money is salvageable. You will come with us and we will be sending you on a commercial flight tomorrow to Miami, Florida. Miguel wants you to know he has already sent your family to the US, and is coordinating with immigration so that you can live there without fear of reprisals.)

The pilot, still in a state of shock, can only nod his head. A few months earlier, he found out that the Blood Alliance Cartel had killed one of his younger brothers because they suspected him of being a snitch. He spent the day with his pregnant wife shopping and was enjoying a quiet dinner at an Italian restaurant in Culiacan. The last supper they shared together on Earth was fortunately pleasant. The excited couple laughed and joked with one another through their meal blissfully ignorant of what awaited them just past the restaurant doors. As they walked together to their car carrying several bags tightly packed with fancy label baby clothes fit for royalty, several men approached them with automatic rifles and opened fire. Their bodies were riddled with lead and a grisly combination of brains and blood poured out into the black asphalt. One of the assassins walked over to the lifeless bodies and put another burst of bullets into each body as a sign of disrespect. It was a horrible end to a lavish evening. It was bound to happen. The assassin then casually strutted off before hopping into a black Mercury sedan with Sinaloa plates. The car sped away disappearing into the dark night.

The local police responded hours later and were unable to find anyone who had witnessed the shooting or was *willing* to admit seeing the killers. They knew no one would ever come forward, since they too would meet the same horrible demise. The bodies were collected unceremoniously and carted to the coroner's office. Family members later claimed the slaughtered remains at the morgue. During the burial, the cemetery was packed with other mourners also burying loved ones. Drug traffickers had killed them ending their lives prematurely. The loud cries could be heard above the roar of backhoes frantically digging graves trying to keep up with the ever-rising murder rate. It was devastating, but Mexican citizens had become more accustomed to dying than living. They were too afraid to genuinely enjoy their lives. The drug violence was morbidly dropping the per capita life span in the country with no end in sight.

The pilot was aware his brother was a money launderer for the cartel, but never fathomed it would lead to his death. He was severely depressed for several days until he began fixating on getting revenge. For many days, he sat at home brooding, his blood boiling… ferocity growing with each passing second. However, no matter how tempestuous he became, he was no match for the professional sicarios working for the cartel. They would snuff him out like a mosquito before he could even *attempt* to avenge the death of his brother. He had seen the battered bodies of those who tried, hanging from bridges by long ropes swaying in the wind like silent wind chimes. Tortured and mutilated human bodies were the symbols of cartel power and viciousness.

The pilot finally decided on his sole course of action and placed a call to the DEA office in Mexico City. He asked the secretary who answered to speak with one of the agents. He was passed on to Villa. The pilot spilled his guts about his past and current role as a transporter of cocaine for the Blood Alliance Cartel. He informed Villa about his pending trip to Colombia and provided detailed information to include the coordinates of the airfield where he would be landing. Villa was also provided the date and estimated time of arrival. After hanging up with the pilot, Villa called his close friend, whom he considered like a brother, General Gallego and provided him with all the details.

Villa closed by saying, "Es bueno escuchar tu voz, mi estimado amigo. Usted ahora tienes toda la información que pude obtener del piloto. Le dije que debía hacer una excusa para alejarse de la pista de aterrizaje poco después de aterrizar el avión. De esa manera, no está en la línea de fuego. También dijo que normalmente la FARC tiene cerca cien of mas de rebeldes bien armados cuando se ha ido a Colombia. Yo no tengo que decir que también tienen granadas propulsadas por cohetes. Se desarrollo cualquier otra información, te llamaré inmediatamente. Lo mejor de la suerte, mi querido amigo." (It's good to hear your voice, my dear friend. You now have all the information I could get from the pilot. I told him he should make an excuse to get away from the runway shortly after landing the plane. Therefore, he will not be in the line of fire. He also said that normally the FARC has about a hundred or more well- armed rebels when he's gone to Colombia to pick up loads of cocaine in the past. I don't have to tell you they also have rocket-propelled grenades. If I develop any other information, I'll call immediately. Best of luck, my dear friend.)

"Mi estimado hermano, aprecio mucho la valiosa información. Viene en un momento oportuno, ya que estamos aumentando nuestros esfuerzos contra los principales carteles y las organizaciones subversivas. Como sabes, las FARC se ajusta tanto a las dos categorías y que ha estado aterrorizando a nuestro país desde 1964. Tenemos que eliminarlos o forzarlos en un tratado de paz. He perdido muchos amigos que han sido asesinados por los rebeldes. Es una situación trágica. Te llamo, mi amigo, una vez que la operación ha terminado. Mi plan es colocar algunos elementos cerca de la pista de aterrizaje un día o dos antes de que llegue el avión. De esta manera sabemos qué esperar. Te envío un abrazo." (My dear brother, I appreciate the valuable information. It comes at an opportune time, as we are increasing our efforts against the major cartels and subversive organizations. As you know the FARC fits into both categories and they have been terrorizing our country since 1964. We have to eliminate them or force them into a peace treaty. I have lost many friends who have been killed by the rebels. It is a tragic situation. I'll call you, my friend, once the operation is over. My plan is to put some scouts near the runway a day or two before the plane arrives. This way we will know what to expect. I send you a hug.)

"Buena suerte y ten cuidado. Espero que tenga una gran victoria!" (Good luck and be careful. I hope you have a great victory!)

General Gallego replied, "Gracias! Vamos a estar en contacto de nuevo, muy pronto. Voy a comenzar a preparar el equipo y mis agentes de policía por la operación. Le garantizo que será un éxito." (Thank you! We'll be in touch again very soon. I will start preparing a team of my police officers for the operation. I guarantee you it will be successful.)

Once the scene at the airstrip is stabilized, one of General Gallego's aids calls Villa and tells him to please hold. A few seconds later, General Gallego's calm voice comes on the line, "Hermano, todo salió como estaba previsto y que ahora están enterrando los cuerpos de los rebeldes en una gran tumba. La cocaína todavía está flotando en el aire y vamos a poder recuperar una gran parte del dinero. Gracias de nuevo. Es sólo a través de la coordinación internacional de que seremos capaces de deshacernos de la amenaza de las drogas ilegales." (Brother, everything went as planned and we are now burying the bodies of the rebels in a single large grave. Cocaine is still floating in the air and we will be able to recover a large part of the money. Thanks again. It is only through international coordination that we will be able to get rid of the threat of illegal drugs.)

"Estoy muy satisfecho de que todo ha ido bien," says Villa, Necesito que les diga a los medios de comunicación que los dos pilotos murieron en la operación. El Cartel Alianza de Sangre van a revisar los periódicos para determinar lo sucedido y tratar de identificar si alguien actuó como informante. Dile al piloto, que una vez que llega a Miami, será recibido por funcionarios de inmigración para darle a él y su familia nuevas identidades para que ahora pueden vivir en paz. Sobre la base de su cooperación, la oficina del Fiscal de EE.UU. no buscará cargos contra él. Tenga cuidado, mi hermano." (I am very pleased that everything went well, Villa says, I need you to tell the media that the two pilots were killed in the operation. The Blood Alliance Cartel will check the newspapers to determine what happened and see if an informant was involved. Tell the pilot that once he arrives in Miami, U.S. immigration officials will meet him. He and his family will be given new identities so they can now live in peace. On the basis of his cooperation, the U.S. Attorney's Office will not seek charges against him. Be careful, my brother.)

"Usted también, mi hermano. Voy a estar aquí durante la mayor parte del día y ha solicitado protección de nuestro ejército en el caso de otras unidades de las FARC deciden contraatacar mientras estamos aquí. La FARC, gracias a ti, tomaron un duro golpe y perdió parte de su gente clave. Más tarde, voy a hacer un informe completo y que le sea enviada a usted para sus archivos." (You too, my brother. I'll be here for most of the day and have requested force protection from our army in the event other FARC units decide to counterattack while we're still here. The FARC, thanks to you, has taken a hard blow and lost some of their key people. Later, I will make a full report that will be sent to you for your records.)

After the call with General Gallego, Villa has Ursula call Ventura on his cell phone. A minute later, Ursula has him on the line. Villa tells him of the operation in Colombia. Ventura, the only one in Mexico who knows of the operation, is elated and congratulates Villa. With a chuckle, he says it would have been humorous to be at the airstrip in Sinaloa to see everyone scatter like cockroaches once they heard what transpired in Colombia. Ventura mentions he will send army units to the airstrip in Mexico and have them drop explosives to blow it up. They will also scare the living shit out of the strip's caretakers.

Ventura changes the subject and informs him they are still in Juarez conducting surveillance on the house where Lisa picked up the money and cocaine. He tells Villa a middle-aged couple has been seen coming and going as if they reside there. They appear to keep a low profile and neither one of them seems to have a job. One of them always remains at the house while the other runs errands. The plan Villa and Ventura developed will move forward the following day by starting a fire in the vacant lot next to the stash house as a ruse. Ventura has already coordinated the operation with a close and trusted friend in the marines. Ventura tells Villa he will call him the following evening after the operation.

The next call Villa makes is to Rafael a/k/a *La Serpiente who is in Culiacan* and cryptically tells him, "Sólo para hacerle saber que la fiesta está prevista para mañana por la noche, pero sé que no puede asistir. Tengo todo listo para usted y su familia a visitar a su tío (EEUU) en el norte. Podría ser una buena idea prepararse para el viaje desde hoy ya que usted sabe cómo la gente puede ser paranoico. Es sólo que no quiero que estés en una situación difícil." (Just to let you know the party is scheduled for tomorrow night, but I know you can't attend. I have everything ready for you and your family to visit your uncle (U.S.) in the north. It might be a good idea to prepare for the trip today since you know how people can get paranoid. I just don't want you in a difficult situation.)

Rafael says, "Gracias por hacérmelo saber. Mi familia es realmente muy contentos de comenzar una nueva vida en los Estados Unidos. La situación en México es cada vez peor. No me preocupo por mí mismo, pero mi familia es inocente. Los traficantes van a ir tras ellos, si no pueden llegar a mí. Muchos funcionarios del gobierno están trabajando con ellos y nadie está seguro. Voy a tener mi familia listo para salir temprano mañana." (Thanks for letting me know. My family is really excited to start a new life in the United States. The situation in Mexico is getting worse. I don't care about myself, but my family is innocent. The traffickers are going to go after them if they can't get to me. Many government officials are working with them and no one is safe. I'll have my family ready to go by early morning.)

"Perfecto! Voy a tener los boletos de avión de Aero-México esperando para que puedan volar directamente a Tucson, Arizona. Sus pasaportes están en orden y agentes de la DEA estarán esperando cuando lleguen allí. Van a vivir en un apartamento, hasta que decidamos dónde van a ir. La inmigración también ayudará a conseguir las identificaciones falsas. Cualquier cosa que hagas, no se comunica con nadie ni se vuelve a México. Entendido?" (Perfect! I'll have AeroMexico airline tickets waiting so you can fly directly to Tucson, Arizona. Your passports are in order and DEA agents will be waiting when you get there. You will live in an apartment until we decide where you will go. Immigration will also help you with false identifications. Whatever you do, don't communicate with anyone or return to Mexico. Understand?)

"Gracias! Vamos a estar listos y comprendo sus instrucciones. Trabajando en el tráfico de drogas con el tiempo te maten y muy pocos son capaces de retirarse. Buena suerte y cuídate," says Rafael. (Thank you! We will be ready and understand your instructions. Working in drug trafficking eventually gets you killed and very few are able to retire. Good luck and take care.)

The following night, two of Ventura's men dressed in black clothes, quietly approach the vacant lot next to the suspected stash house in Juarez. They carry a red five-gallon can of gasoline and crouch in the tall weeds. They move slowly, a few feet at a time, perspiring heavily, not as a result of the warm temperature, but because they're nervous that someone will later identify them. They know that if they are identified as being part of the operation, the Cartel of the North will waste no time in putting out a death contract on them that will make the recent Metal Coffin murders look like a kiddie ride at Disneyland. As luck will have it, the wind is moving east to west, which means the fire will travel toward the suspected cartel stash house. Rapidly, they douse a patch of weeds with the pungent smelling gas. One of them retrieves a cigarette lighter from his pants pocket and tries to light it. It is not working. He feels panic and his mouth goes completely dry. A deep sense of relief comes over him when his companion pulls out a book of matches from his shirt. The first match ignites and it is flung into the gasoline soaked weeds. A loud whooshing sound can be heard as the fire sucks in oxygen and spreads rapidly across the yard. Ventura's men sprint across the field with the empty gas can until they reach a waiting blue Buick sedan and jump in the back seat. They take deep breaths and their hands continue to shake nervously. Now, comes the hard part – to wait patiently.

Ventura, sees the fire blazing from a distance, and calls the marine commander and says one word, "Showtime."

Three camouflaged-painted Dodge RAM trucks with mounted M2 .50 caliber machine guns roll out into the street with squealing tires in front of the expanding fire. The combined heat from the weather, fire, and overall tension is oppressive. The men are focused willing to engage in violent actions if it is warranted. Ventura and his men watch as twenty marines in gray uniforms, heavily armed with AR-15s, leap from the trucks and race towards the stash house. They bang on the door with their rifle butts hard and heavy. A man, bald, heavy set, with thick chest hair answers the door wearing a faded, blue bathrobe and flip-flops. A woman, presumably his wife, a small redhead with bright red lipstick curiously peeks out from behind him. When she sees the inferno in the next lot engulfing everything in its path and coming in their direction, she screams in fear and desperately pleads to the men at the door and to the Virgin Mary for the fire to be put out before it reaches their house. They identify themselves as Felipe and Rachel Arteaga. Playing his role perfectly, the marine Captain tells them to step into the street for their safety and that the fire department has been advised and is on its way.

Several marines are sent into the stash house under the pretext of helping anyone else who is inside. This leads to even more screaming and protests from the Arteagas. The marines move fast and efficiently into the residence and spread out into the different rooms.

As one of them walks on the hardwood flooring in the living room, he hears a loud, suspicious creak. He lifts a circular, red Persian rug, and discovers a small trapdoor on the floor. When he opens it, he discovers the entrance to a large cavern underneath the house. His flashlight illuminates the area and he is stunned by what he sees. There are hundreds of white bales neatly stacked on top of each other. Next to them are large blue plastic barrels sealed with thick, gray duct tape. He is literally looking at the mother lode of all drug seizures in history. He excitedly runs out of the house to tell his Captain about his discovery. As he's passing the information to his Captain, three large fire trucks arrive with sirens blaring. The firemen quickly begin pulling the long, heavy-duty hoses and turn on the water. The strong torrential spray of water rapidly extinguishes the fire, but smoke begins to envelop the area like an ominous dark cloud. The screeches and expletives by the Arteagas continue and are almost loud enough to drown out the deafening sounds of the fire trucks.

The marine whispers in his Captain's ear, "Jefe, usted tiene que entrar en la casa y ver esto por sí mismo. Hay una enorme caverna bajo de la casa. Está lleno de costales y una gran cantidad de barriles de plástico de gran tamaño." (Boss, you have to enter the house and see this for yourself. There is a huge cavern beneath the house. It is full of bales and a lot of large plastic barrels.)

The Captain orders his men to hang on to the Arteagas who are now hysterical. The couple begins threatening the marines telling them of the heavy price they will pay once they call their friends in high places. They vehemently object to the marines searching their house without a warrant. The Captain smiles and reminds them they are in Mexico and not in the United States. He doesn't give a shit about the Arteagas' so-called *rights* and smugly tells them it is the responsibility of the Marines to protect lives, therefore they are within their authority to search the house to make sure no one else is trapped inside. He suddenly rears back and punches Felipe in the face with his huge fist and tells him to shut the fuck up. Felipe whimpers and lowers his head in submission. He knows any further emotional outbursts or threats will lead to a beating he may not survive.

The Captain and a handful of his men walk in the house and make their way down a narrow ladder into the dark cavern. They use their flashlights for illumination since it is completely devoid of light. A marine use a sharp bayonet to cut into one of the bales and several kilo-sized packages tumble onto the dirt floor. He scoops one up and pierces it with his knife. White powder spills out and a field test confirms it is cocaine. They count six hundred bales, each one containing twenty kilos. They estimate it is about twelve metric tons of cocaine, worth hundreds of millions of dollars. Next they pull the tape from one of the plastic barrels, which astonishingly is stuffed with U.S. currency. The denominations range from twenty to one hundred dollar notes. The money is wrapped in clear plastic and sealed with transparent tape. The Captain counts a hundred and ten barrels. Someone is really going to be fucking pissed off because of this seizure, he thinks. He removes his cell from his pocket and calls Ventura to come to the scene. It takes all but a few minutes when he and his men arrive at the house. Ventura goes in alone and the Captain proudly shows him their significant discovery. Ventura's first words are, "Hijo de puta, esto es como ganar la lotería. Tenemos que conseguir algunos camiones grandes para mover todo este dinero y la cocaína antes de que el Cártel del Norte se entere. Voy a dejar que hagas eso y voy a interrogar a la pareja dentro de la casa para ver qué más saben." (Son of a whore, this is like winning the lottery. We need to get some big trucks to move all this money and cocaine before the Cartel of the North finds out.

I'll let you do that and I will question the couple living in the house to see what else they know.)

"Voy a conseguir algunos de nuestros camiones pesados y mas personnal aquí tan pronto como sea posible. Además, voy a establecer un perímetro de seguridad alrededor de la area. Será cerrado apretado que una lata," says the Captain. (I'll get some of our heavy trucks and some more personnel over here as soon as possible. I'll establish a security perimeter around the area too. It will be sealed tighter than a steel drum.)

Ventura's men escort the Arteagas into the house and put them in separate rooms. Fear is written on their faces and they know what is coming and it is not going to be pleasant. They are laid on their backs and their hands and feet are bound with electrical cords ripped from the lamps in the house. Meantime one of the agents goes to the trunk of Ventura's car and pulls out a case of Tehuacán mineral water in glass bottles. He also takes out something more sinister, a long, black cylindrical object. It is an evil looking electric cattle prod with two electrodes at the end. It is the prime interrogation tool of choice for Mexico's security forces. Ventura starts with Felipe who is now sobbing like a baby looking at the ceiling expecting his maker to save him or at least take him to paradise quickly.

Ventura peppers him with questions, "A quien le pertenece todo el dinero y cocaína? Cuánto tiempo ha vivido en esta casa? Dime la cantidad de cocaína y dinero en la caverna? (To whom does all the money and cocaine belong to? How long have you lived in this house? What is the amount of cocaine and money in the cave?)

Felipe swallows hard and replies, "Señor, no sé lo que está hablando. Mi esposa y yo sólo alquilamos esta casa y no sabían que había drogas y el dinero debajo de la casa. Somos víctimas inocentes. Por favor, señor, usted tiene que creerme." (Sir, I don't know what you're talking about. My wife and I just rent this house and didn't know about the drugs and money under the house. We are innocent victims. Please, sir, you have to believe me.)

"Crees que soy estúpido. Es eso lo que me está diciendo? Usted dice que no sabe nada y uno de los marinos sin mirar por otra cosa que mas gente en la casa, encuentra la caleta. Realmente me decepcionó y me hace muy molesto. Veremos lo que sabes." (Do you think I'm stupid? Is that what you're telling me? You say you know nothing and one of the Marines without looking for anything other than more people in the house finds the stash. I am really disappointed and it makes me very upset. We will see what you know.)

Ventura has two of his agents pull Felipe's blue jeans and underwear down to his knees and then takes a bottle of water and douses his genitals. He then lifts the chicharra over Felipe's head so he can see it and flips on the switch. A wicked, white electrical current can be seen rapidly moving towards the electrodes. Ventura deftly places the electrodes into Felipe's wet crotch. A gruesome shriek comes from his mouth that twists in agony and he literally catapults a foot off the ground while lying flat on his back. He begins to sweat profusely and he knows the torture is only going to get worse. Ventura shoves the chicharra into his numb genitals and another blast of hot electricity shoots violently through his body. He convulses and all of his muscles tighten causing tremendous stress to the entire body. The water acts as a conduit for the electric current making it more powerful. Felipe screams for mercy, but he knows it is futile. He surrenders to the inevitable.

He groans, "Señor, se lo ruego no más, no más, por favor! Te diré todo lo que sé. Esta es almacenamiento primario utilizado por el Cartel del Norte. Crecí con Albino Romero y fuimos juntos a la escuela. Él sabía que yo no tenía mucho dinero y él me ofreció un trabajo para proporcionar seguridad a sus drogas y dinero. En realidad sólo vivo aquí con mi esposa y se aseguró de que nadie entre en la casa. El me llamaba cuando Lisa o otras persona iban a venir a recoger parte de la cocaína o dinero. Me paga cuatro mil dólares al mes por mis servicios." (Sir, I beg no more, no more, please! I'll tell you everything I know. This is the primary drug and money storage area used by the Cartel of the North. I grew up with Albino Romero and we went to school together. He knew I didn't have much money and he offered me a job to provide security to his drugs and money. I really only live here with my wife to make sure no one breaks into the house. He always calls and lets me know when Lisa or someone else is coming to pick up some of the cocaine or money. I am paid four thousand U.S. dollars a month for my services.) Ventura asks him, "Cuánto dinero y cocaína hay aquí? (How much money and cocaine are here?)

"Hay un poco más de doce toneladas de cocaína y trescientos millones de dólares. Creo que las cantidades son actuales y que equilibran los totales cada semana. Una parte de las ganancias se utiliza para pagar el soborno a políticos y también para comprar armas en los EE.UU. Cada año, el Cartel del Norte hace cientos de millones de dólares y es imposible para el lavado de toda ella." (There is a little over twelve tons of cocaine and three hundred million dollars. I think the numbers are current because the totals are balanced each week. A portion of the proceeds is used to pay bribes to politicians and to buy weapons in the U.S. Each year the Cartel of the North makes hundreds of millions of dollars and it is impossible to launder all of it.)

Ventura forces the issue, "Así que usted está en contacto directo con Romero? Estoy dispuesto a hacer un trato con usted. Si se comunica con Romero y hacer que él se reúnen en la ciudad donde lo podemos arrestar, vamos a dejar que usted y su esposa ir libre. De lo contrario, ambos van a pasar el resto de sus vidas en la cárcel. Ha llegado el momento para que usted pueda hacer una decisión." (So you are in direct contact with Romero? I am willing to make a deal with you. If you communicate with Romero and get him to meet you in the city where we can arrest him, we will let you and your wife go free. Otherwise, both of you are going to spend the rest of your lives in jail. The time has come for you to make a decision.)

After the two painful shots of electricity, Felipe is trying to be rational even though his thought process is totally scrambled with pain. He fights hard to use common sense since neither of the two options has a silver lining. He knows that if he helps with the capture of Romero, the cartel sicarios will be unleased and they will not rest until he is dead. On the other hand, he knows he will not survive in prison. He finally makes the decision to turn in his friend to buy his freedom. Treason, he knows, is the cornerstone of drug trafficking anyway. Honor is not part of the equation.

"Voy a ayudarle a obtener Romero, pero usted tendrá que darme algo de dinero para poder escondernos en Europa. Vamos a tener que salir de México, ya que la mafia aquí no perdona u olvida las transgresiones. Esa es mi única condición para que te ayude." (I'll help you get Romero, but you have to give me some money to hide in Europe. We'll have to leave Mexico because the mafia here does not forgive or forget transgressions. That is my only condition to help you.)

Ventura says, "Bueno, voy a darle trescientos mil dólares de los dinero que pertenece a Romero. Eso le dará un nuevo comienzo en la vida, pero tendrá que ocultar para el resto de sus vidas. Es irónico que Romero será realmente el que va a pagar por su captura." (Well, I'll give you three hundred thousand dollars of the money belonging to Romero. That will give you a new start in life, but you'll have to hide for the rest of your lives. It is ironic that Romero will actually be the one to pay you for his capture.)

"Tenemos un trato! Tan pronto como se ha terminado, tiene que darme el dinero y mi esposa y yo estaremos en el próximo avión a España. Romero confía en mí con su vida. No me gusta hacer esto a él, pero es una cuestión de él o yo." (We have a deal! As soon as it is over, you will have to give me the money and my wife and I will be on the next plane to Spain. Romero trusts me with his life. I do not like doing this to him, but it is a question of him or me.)

Ventura asks, "Qué es lo que haces cuando quiere reunirse con Romero? También hay un lugar específico donde se encuentran? Usted utiliza códigos cuando se comunica con él? También necesito saber cuántos de sus sicarios viajan con él y los tipos de armas que por lo general llevan? No se puede dejar de lado ningún detalle porque si usted arruina intencionalmente la reunión, yo personalmente voy a poner una bala en tu cabeza." (What do you do when you want to meet with Romero? Also is there a specific place where you meet? Do you use codes when communicating with him? I also need to know how many of his hitmen travel with him and the types of weapons they usually carry? You cannot leave out any details because if you intentionally ruin the meeting, I am personally going to put a bullet in your head.)

"Normalmente nos encontramos en una de sus muchas casas de seguridad que tiene en toda la ciudad. Nunca mencionamos direcciones, pero los códigos que designan la ubicación. Por ejemplo, si queremos encontrar a su lugar favorito, decimos que vamos a vernos en la pizzería. Cada lugar tiene un nombre en clave. Romero viaja con no más de seis sicarios, ya que no quiere llamar la atención con un grupo mas grande. Los sicarios son generalmente armados con AK-47's y AR-15s. Pero también llevan pistolas. Ellos están fuertemente armados y algunas veces tienen unas granadas de mano. Sus sicarios están bien entrenados. El trajo un grupo de ex-soldados de las fuerzas especiales de Israel a entrenarlos en tácticas militares." (We usually meet in one of his many safehouses he has throughout the city. We never mention addresses, but use the codes that designate the location. For example, if we want to meet at his favorite place, we say that we will meet at the pizzeria. Each place has a code name. Romero travels with no more than six hitmen because he does not want to draw attention with a larger group. The gunmen are usually armed with AK-47s and AR-15s. But they also carry handguns. They are heavily armed and sometimes have some hand grenades. His hitmen are well trained. He brought a group of ex-soldiers from the Israeli Special Forces to train them in military tactics.)

Ventura reflects for a moment and then gives him instructions on what to tell Romero. He goes over the story with him several times so he does not make a mistake that will tip off Romero. He also has to make sure that he is calm and not overly nervous when he makes the call. Ventura knows that Romero is extremely cunning and will pick up on signs when something is not right. He also has Felipe drink two shots of tequila to settle his nerves.

Felipe dials a number on his cell phone and says, "Tío, hemos tenido algunos problemas aquí en la casa. Un incendio se inició al lado y una rutina de patrulla marína vio y respondió. Tenían miedo de que el fuego podia llegar a nuestra casa y nos sacaron, pero ellos entraron para ver si había alguien más en el interior. Les dije que no había nadie más, pero entraron de todos modos. Encontraron lo que teníamos en la casa. El comandante está dispuesto a negociar con nosotros y llegar a un acuerdo. Él sabe que nosotros le daremos más compensación que el gobierno. Tenemos que vernos para que podamos discutir los detalles. En la pizzería? (Uncle, we had some problems here at the house. A fire broke out next door and a marine routine patrol saw it and responded. They were afraid that the fire would reach our house so they evacuated us, but then they went in to see if anyone else was inside. I told them that there was no one else, but they entered anyway. They found what we had in the house. The Captain is willing to negotiate with us and reach an agreement. He knows that we will give him more compensation than the government. We have to meet so we can discuss the details. At the pizzeria?)

Romero screams, "Hijos de puta, voy a decapitar a todos! Todos sus familias también serán asesinados de la misma forma, incluidos los padres, hijos y esposas. Inicialmente, pagaré, porque no tengo otra opción, pero más tarde todos ellos van a morir. Ellos han iniciado una reacción en cadena donde va correr más sangre que el Río Grande tiene agua. Nos encontraremos en la pizzería en cuatro horas. Asegúrese de que no te sigan." (Sons of whores, I will decapitate them all! All their families will also be killed in the same way, including parents, children, and wives. Initially, I will pay because I have no other choice, but later they will all die. They have started a chain reaction where more blood will flow than the Rio Grande has water. We will meet at the pizzeria in four hours. Make sure you are not followed.) This was a ruse since only the police and marines would go to the safe house and hope Romero showed up. Felipe would remain in custody.

After hanging up with Romero, Felipe gives Ventura the address of the location code named pizzeria. It is close to the center of the city in a residential area where people mind their own business. The address is Calle Paraguey No. 870 Sur, Esquina Jose Barunda, Colonia Partido Romero, Juarez, 32177. Felipe describes it as a white colonial style house with a large garden and a metal gate in front. Felipe tells Ventura they need to take heavy sledge hammers since the doors are reinforced with steel bars. Ventura dispatches most of his men to the location so they can find good vantage points from which they can conduct surveillance without being detected. The marine Captain also sends some of his troops who will be at a safe distance since they are highly visible with their military trucks and uniforms.

With the trap being set, Ventura calls Villa on his cell. He tells him of the seizure and the operation to lure Romero to one of his safe houses where they stand a reasonable chance of capturing him. Villa tells him that Lisa will probably be with him and it is important to try to take her alive. She knows the total infrastructure of the cartel probably better than anyone, including Romero. If they can get her to flip, she can help destroy the cartel. Ventura said they will try, but can't guarantee it. Villa wishes his friend luck. Drug lords are fiercely protected by loyal sicarios who are willing to give up their lives to save them. For them, it is a badge of honor to die in a hail of bullets because it shows they have balls.

It is decided that the marine Captain will remain at the house until reinforcements arrive. Ventura also leaves one of his men to watch the Arteagas. He is not going to take Felipe to the site, but tells him if Romero calls, he is to tell him that he is on his way. Ventura checks his AK-47 in the trunk of the car. He has two banana clips taped to each other so he can quickly flip the other once the bullets in the first one are expended. Ventura has learned several tactics, which give him a distinct advantage in life and death situations. On operations, a matter of seconds can make the difference between surviving or not. He puts the assault rifle in the front seat and three of his men also carrying long weapons jump in the car with him.

Ventura gets on the radio, "Estoy en camino a la ubicación. Han encontrado un lugar para ver la casa? Ustedes tiene que asegurarse de que no pueden ser visto. Uno de ustedes debe ser capaz de ver la casa. Una vez que nuestros *amigos* llegan tenemos que rodear la casa rápidamente. Ten cuidado." (I'm on my way to the location. Have you found a place where you can see the house? You have to make sure you cannot be seen. One of you needs be able to see the house. Once our *friends* arrive we need to surround the house quickly. Be careful.)

The radio crackles, "Sí, señor, estamos en posición y puedo ver la entrada principal de la casa. José está cubriendo la entrada trasera. Afortunadamente, teníamos un poco de tiempo para encontrar lugares en los que no serán capaces de vernos. Nuestras radios están funcionando bien y estamos listos con nuestras armas y chalecos antibalas." (Yes, Sir, we are in position and I can see the main entrance of the house. Jose is covering the rear entrance. Fortunately, we had a little time to find places where they will not be able to see us. Our radios are working well and we are ready with our guns and bulletproof vests.)

Ventura clicks on his radio transmitter button, "Alguien tiene un almádena y una larga barra de hierro para que podamos entrar en la casa en poco tiempo? El tiempo va a ser crítico porque nuestro "amigo" puede tener túneles u otras vías de escape." (Does someone have a sledgehammer and a long metal bar so that we can enter the house quickly? Time will be critical because our "friend" can have tunnels or other escape routes.)

"Comandante, tengo algunas esas herramientas en la cahuela de nuestro coche desde nuestra última incursión. Tenemos algunas granadas de aturdimiento que Villa nos dio. Cuando abrimos la puerta, podemos echarlos en la casa y desorientar a ellos. Estamos listos para el asalto de la casa cuando lo órdenes." (Commander, I have some of these tools in the trunk of my car since our last raid. We have some stun grenades that Villa gave us as well. When we open the door, we can throw them into the house and disorient them. We are ready for the assault of the house upon your orders.)

Ventura calmly replies, "Muy bien, tu y los hombres contigo van a ir conmigo a la puerta de enfrente. Nuestros amigos de la marina estan una distancia más lejos de nosotros y tenemos que coordinar un asalto simultáneo. Avisame cuando vea cualquier movimiento en la casa. Nuestro *amigo* siente que es dueño de la ciudad, por lo demás todo el estado. Su arrogancia será su caída." (Very good, you and the men with you will go with me to the front door. Our friends from the marines will be a distance farther away from us and we have to coordinate a simultaneous assault. Let me know when you see any movement in the house. Our *friend* feels he owns the city, and quite frankly all of the state. Arrogance will be his downfall.)

A strong wind comes through violently sweeping the dusty street and dark clouds began to form in the sky. Ventura and his men are as restless as a coiled rattlesnake ready to sink its poisonous fangs into its prey. The waiting just before a dangerous operation is incredibly miserable. Time moves very slowly and so many thoughts go through ones mind that the brain can't process them all. Worse, it is hard to sit still in a car while huge amounts of adrenaline move ferociously through your body. Despite all your planning, something will inevitably go wrong, which can fuck everything. Murphy's Law is always present and you have to be able to make rapid changes during the execution of operations.

Each car that comes down the street is carefully scrutinized, with everyone hoping that Romero has arrived, but no, they keep going. Finally, they see a black Mercedes Benz SUV come down the street and go past the house. Five minutes later, it appears on the opposite side of the street and momentarily stops in front of the safe house. It then quickly drives away and returns a minute later. They are obviously doing a security sweep before the drug kingpin comes into the area. The SUV finally stops and a short, stocky man in a black cowboy hat and boots steps out and walks to the door. He seems to be unlocking it. Meantime, the SUV drives away and continues to drive back and forth on the street. Another half hour goes by, which seems like an eternity, when two gray Chevrolet Tahoe's drive slowly and cautiously down the street. Both come to a stop and seven men and a woman walk rapidly into the house.

The radio sputters and one of Ventura's men says, "Comandante, hay siete hombres y una mujer que acaban de entrar. Uno de los hombres es sin duda es nuestro *amigo* y la mujer parece ser Lisa. Un par de hombres regresaron a los Tahoes y están llevando grandes bolsas a la casa. Vi un barril que sobresale de uno de ellos. Son armas largas." (Commander, there are seven men and one woman who have just entered. One of the men is definitely our *friend* and the woman appears to be Lisa. A couple of men have returned to the Tahoes and are carrying large bags into the house. I saw a barrel sticking out from one of them. They are long weapons.)

"Está bien, asaltamos la casa en cinco minutos, que será tiempo suficiente para que la marina llegue. José, usted y sus hombres cubrirá la parte posterior de la casa, Jairo y Juan, ustedes y sus hombres estarán a los lados de la casa. Los marines le ayudará. Yo y los otros a derribar la puerta delantera." (Okay, we will assault the house in five minutes, which will be enough time for the marines to arrive. Jose, you and your men cover the back of the house, Juan and Jairo, you and your men will cover the sides of the house. The marines will help you. The others and I will break down the front door.)

The tension reaches a super high level and beads of sweat forms on the foreheads of each man. They know the dangers, but are willing to risk their lives for a greater cause. They take solace in knowing *a hero only dies once but a coward dies a thousand deaths*. It is now all in the roll of the dice.

They grab their weapons and make sure a round is chambered and ready for action. They squeeze their weapons hard to release some of the tension.

Ventura suddenly yells into the radio, "Adelante, hombres y vayan con Dios. Que nadie escapar de la trampa." (Forward, men and go with God. Let no one escape the trap.)

Car doors can be heard slamming and then the rhythm of stomping boots moving swiftly across the street. Ventura reaches the door first and takes the sledgehammer from one of his men and begins to viciously pound the front door. It buckles but doesn't open. Suddenly, a repetitive pop, pop, pop, of gunfire comes from inside the house. Just in the nick of time, one of the marine trucks rolls in front of the house and opens up with a thunderous roar from a .50 caliber machine gun. Ventura and his men hit the floor as the shower of hot lead shatters the windows and splinters the walls above their heads. Meantime, two of the sicarios attempt to run out the back door and a burst from Jose's AK-47 shoves them lifeless back through the door. Ventura stands up again and begins to wedge the long metal bar into the door and pulls hard again and again. Finally, a loud bang and the door pops wide open. One of Ventura's men yanks the pins on two stun grenades and tosses them inside. The explosions are thunderous. Ventura and a few of his men crouch low then run inside firing their weapons. One of the sicarios charges out of room and fires a volley of bullets, which strike the man behind Ventura in the face and neck. It completely obliterates his head. He never knew what hit him. Ventura fires back and six rounds hit the sicario's chest, which spins him around and he drops face down onto the floor.

Someone yells from one of the rooms, "Nos rendimos! No dispares estamos saliendo desarmados." (We surrender! Do not shoot we are coming out unarmed.)

Ventura says, "Salgan uno a la vez con las manos en el aire. No hagan ningún movimiento brusco." (Come out one at a time with your hands in the air. Do not make any sudden movements.)

Three men come out and are quickly handcuffed. A sweep of the house reveals that four sicarios have been killed in the horrendous shootout. Ventura is distraught one of his men has been killed and feels like killing the rest of the traffickers, but he knows revenge will not bring his colleague back. The amount of blood makes the floors extremely slippery.

One of Ventura's men yells, "Comandante, tienes que ver esto. Hay un mecanismo hidráulico que se abre y entra en el sistema de drenaje de la ciudad." (Commander, you have to see this. There is a hydraulic mechanism that opens and goes into city's the drainage system.)

Ventura enters the living room and sees a small, coffee table about twelve inches off the floor on one end. He notices hydraulic lifts had started to lift the table but then apparently jammed, preventing the men from escaping. Twelve inches is not nearly enough room for them to squeeze through, but it is for a thin female. Lisa has escaped into the city's drainage system. Ventura goes back to where the three men are being held and his gaze meets that of Romero, one of the most feared drug lords in Mexico.

They stare down each other for a minute and then Romero tells him, "Puedo tener una palabra con usted?" (Can I have a word with you?)

Ventura quietly pulls him aside. Romero looks him squarely in the eye and says, "Si me liberas, te haré uno de los hombres más ricos de todo México. Si decide no hacerlo, entonces usted es un hombre muerto caminando y voy a matar a todos los de su familia. Una cárcel es sólo una cosa temporal para mí de todos modos. Necesito su respuesta ahora." (If you release me, I will make you one of the richest men in Mexico. If you choose not to, then you are a dead man walking and I will kill all your family. A prison is only a temporary thing for me anyway. I need your answer now.)

Ventura smiles, "Cree que me puede sobornar con su sucio, dinero de sangre por lo qual ha matado a miles de personas? Si tocas un solo pelo de uno de los miembros de mi familia voy a tener que usar una sierra de cadena para hacer filetes de ti para los perros del vecindario. (Do you think you can bribe me with your dirty blood money for which you have killed thousands of people? If you touch a single hair on the head of anyone in my family, I'll use a chainsaw to make steaks out of you for the neighborhood dogs.)

Ventura calls out to one of his men, "Hay que transportar a todos ellos al aeropuerto. Voy a conseguir uno de nuestros aviones para transportarlos a la prisión de máxima seguridad en la Ciudad de México. Si los dejamos en la zona, los sueltan por la mañana. Vamos a dejar el dinero y la cocaína con la marina y podemos asegurarlo en su base. Podemos quemar la cocaína despues y el procurador general de México puede decidir lo que quieren hacer con el dinero. Quiero que algunos de los hombres buscan a Lisa y ver si podemos encontrarla." (Transport them all to the airport. I'll get one of our planes to transport them to the maximum security prison in Mexico City. If we leave them in the area, they will be re-

184 Michael S. Vigil

leased by tomorrow morning. Let's leave the money and cocaine with the marines; they can secure it at their base. We
can burn the cocaine later and the Attorney General of Mexico can decide what to do with money. I want some of the
men to look for Lisa and see if we can find her.)

Villa receives a call from Ventura who gives him the
good news. Both are ecstatic and congratulate each other.
The well planned strategy of meeting with Lisa in an undercover capacity and the effective use of technology has allowed them to locate the principal stash site of the Cartel of
the North. The operation has resulted in the seizure of twelve
tons of cocaine that won't reach the U.S. market and the
three hundred million dollars that will not be used to buy
weapons or corrupt public officials. More importantly, one
of the most powerful traffickers in the world is now in custody. It is a win-win situation all the way around.

The Arteaga's are given their money and they immediately leave Mexico. They are small fish and are used as nothing more than a hook to capture the big prize, Albino
Romero. Rafael, a/k/a *La Serpiente,* is now safely in the U.S.
with his family. Villa and Ventura agree that Lisa will probably now take the reins of the cartel while Romero is in
prison. Of concern is the massive corruption in the Mexican
prison system and Romero has unlimited power and wealth.
He still has the full support of his cartel's infrastructure.
Villa knows the U.S. will seek his extradition, but that can
take several years. Romero has the best attorneys money can
buy and they will continue to file amparos (legal injunctions)
to prevent it.

Several months later, Romero is sentenced to forty years
in prison for drug trafficking and money laundering. Unfortunately, he is not convicted for the thousands of murders his

cartel has committed. Villa knows that ninety-eight percent of the murders in Mexico go unsolved. Most of them are investigated by corrupt municipal and state police forces. Romero controls them all in the northern part of Mexico. He is their paymaster and puppeteer who pulled their strings.

CHAPTER 9

The Stewmaker

t is a warm, dusty day and a strong mountain wind blows past Atenco's safehouse near the border between Sinaloa and Durango. Sitting outside, he surveys his isolated, desolate kingdom. He is accompanied by some of his most trusted sicarios, to include La Sombra. Still seething in anger over the money he lost in Colombia, he is relieved he didn't have to pay for the tons of cocaine, which were destroyed in the police raid. There is an unwritten rule that if the cocaine hadn't yet left Colombia and is seized or destroyed by the local police or military, the Mexican traffickers aren't responsible for it. The loss is that of the Colombians because it had not yet been handed over to the Mexicans.

Atenco addresses La Sombra, "El que fue responsable de mí perder los millones de dólares en Colombia me va pagar con su vida. Hemos estado tomando demasiados golpes y no podemos permitir más. Necesitamos ampliar nuestro negocio para cubrir las pérdidas y ahora es el momento de hacerlo. Romero ha sido capturado y su cártel ahora es débil. Esa perra que el ama, Lisa, se ha hecho cargo de él. Ella no tiene las bolas como un hombre." (Whoever was responsible for me losing millions of dollars in Colombia will pay me with his life. We've been taking too many blows and we cannot afford more. We need to expand our business to cover our recent losses and now is the time to do it. Romero has been captured and his cartel is now weak. That bitch he loves, Lisa, has taken charge of the cartel, at least temporarily. She doesn't have balls like a man.)

Everyone roared with laughter and La Sombra spoke, "Sí, estoy de acuerdo que el Cártel del Norte es ahora débil, pero Romero va a sobornar a los funcionarios de prision para que pueda controlar su organización desde el interior de la prisión. Estoy seguro de que le darán acceso a teléfonos celulares y sus asociados. No es la situación óptima, pero es lo mejor que tiene ahora. Tenemos que presionar el ataque a su cartel y si podemos matar a Lisa, pierde la persona más leal y de confianza que tiene en su organization." (Yes, I agree that the Cartel of the North is now weak, but Romero will bribe prison officials so he can control his organization from inside prison. I'm sure they will give him access to cell phones and to his associates. Not the best situation, but it is the best he has now. We have to press the attack on his cartel and if we can kill Lisa, he loses the most loyal and trustworthy person in his organization.)

Atenco responds, "Muy cierto, tenemos que avanzar de manera agresiva. Ellos van a estar desorientado durante un tiempo y tenemos que tomar ventaja de esa situación. Ahora es el momento de hacerse cargo de su ruta en los EE.UU y estoy hablando del corredor Juárez a El Paso. Calculo podemos aumentar nuestros ingresos a la mitad de mil millones de dólares al año si es nuestro. (Very true, we need to move aggressively. They will be disoriented for a while and we have to take advantage of that situation. Now is the time to take control of their routes into the U.S. and I'm talking about the Juarez to El Paso corridor. I estimate we can increase our revenues by half a billion dollars a year if it is ours.

A week later, Atenco and La Sombra flood the city of Juarez with an army of their most vicious sicarios. They already had weapons in the area and decided to operate out of a ranch south of the city. They set up a large security perimeter making it impossible for anyone to gain the element of surprise. La Sombra told them that they needed to kill all the corrupt politicians that protected Romero's organization. The first targets they would go after would be the mayor and the local chief of police.

Early one morning, Jacobo Montes, the Juarez Chief of Police awakes and sleepily gets into the shower. He will have a busy day, a meeting with his staff and later a speech to a local business group. He brushes his gold-capped teeth and combs the few strands of hair that remain on his head. He also runs the comb a couple of times through his Emiliano Zapate style mustache. He sits on the bed and finally squeezes into his uniform pants, which are at least two sizes too small. Montes spits on his black shoes and rubs them with the sleeve of his shirt in order to make them looked polished. It doesn't work. He is happy and starts to hum the song, *La Paloma*.

His wife of thirty years, Olga, yells at him from the next room, "Cállate! Estás asustando a los putos perros afuera. No puedes oírlos llorando de dolor? Si va a cantar, hacerlo en el medio del puto desierto." (Shut up! You're scaring the fucking dogs. Can you not hear them crying in pain? If you are going to sing, do it in the middle of the fucking desert.)

"Mi amor, yo soy muy feliz hoy. Me pagan hoy la gente de Romero y me deben mucho dinero. Este es el dinero que uso para comprarte cosas bonitas. No podía hacer eso con mi pinche sueldo. Deberías estar feliz." (My love, I am very happy. Romero's people pay me today and they owe me a lot of money. This is money that I use to buy you pretty things. I could not do that with my fucking salary. You should be happy.)

Olga enters the room in a red silk bathrobe that shows the curvature of her body. Her skin is dark and she has jet-black hair. Jacobo is many years her senior and it shows. Olga tries to act cultured, but has the mouth of a drunken sailor. He is worse and has the manners of a Neanderthal.

Olga looks at him with contempt, "Pinche idiota, hay que darse cuenta de que nada en esta vida es gratis. Ellos te están pagando con dinero ahora, pero el tiempo vendrá cuando te pagarán con plomo. Usted es nada para ellos. Me sorprende que usted todavía está vivo." (Fucking idiot, you have to realize that nothing in life is free. They are paying with money now, but the time will come when you will be paid with lead. You are nothing to them. I am surprised that you are still alive.)

Jacobo frowns and says, "Por supuesto que me necesitan! Yo protejo sus operaciones y no podían funcionar sin mí. Los carteles no pueden existir sin gente como yo para ayudarlos. Seria imposible. Ellos lo saben y es por eso que me pagan mucho dinero. El gobierno nos da salarios de miseria." (Of course they need me! I protect their operations and they could not function without me. The cartels cannot exist without people like me helping them. It would be impossible. They know it and that's why they pay me a lot of money. The government gives us poverty wages.)

She replies, "Jacobo, eres estúpido! Hay otros carteles que son enemigos de Romero y su organización. Te van a matar como una pulga porque trabajas para un cartel rival. Es necesario que examinen su puto cerebro." (Jacobo, you are stupid! There are other cartels that are enemies of Romero and his organization. They'll kill you like a flea because you work for a rival cartel. You need to get your fucking brain examined.)

Jacobo shrugs his head in submission and straps the holster with his .45 caliber Colt handgun to his waist and adjusts it so it hangs like that of an old western gunslinger. He fancies himself as Clint Eastwood in one of his spaghetti westerns. He grabs his paper bag with the usual two ham sandwiches and a bag of barbeque flavored potato chips. Jacobo tries to give his wife a kiss on the cheek, but she pulls away in disgust. He swallows hard with eyes downcast and walks out the door. He approaches the door of his unmarked police car, a Ford Bronco, when he hears the screech of tires nearby. Alarmed, he quickly turns and sees several armed men jump from two dark cars with AK-47s. He reaches for his gun and fumbles it. The last thing he sees is his gun tumbling in the air towards the ground. Loud explosions are heard as bullets rip into him and tumble through his body, tearing flesh and splintering bone. He groans and stumbles backward. One of the sicarios moves forward with a boomerang shaped Gurkha kukri fourteen-inch knife. Two other men lift Jacobo into a sitting position. The man with the knife slides it swiftly from left to right across his throat. Blood splashes everywhere and the sicario holds the severed head in his hand when Olga walks out the front door. She screams in horror and the sicario turns and throws Jacobo's head at her like it was a basketball. Her screams become louder and she falls to her knees. The sicarios smirk and one of them yells, "pinche puta." They get into their cars and speed away.

Less than seventy-two hours later, the mayor of Juarez, Benjamin Turbay, is speeding on the road back to Juarez from Chihuahua, Chihuahua. He had met with the governor on infrastructure development issues regarding the state. Turbay, in his black pinstripe suit and red tie, is in a convoy of five cars. He has twenty state police officers with him and has two cars in front and two in back. He is in the middle car. Turbay became mayor two years earlier with the financial support of the Cartel of the North. He is now a wealthy man and has a beautiful wife. He is heavy set, with protruding eyes that make him look like a frog.

He tells one of his bodyguards, "El gobernador de mierda siempre me está molestando en temas estúpidos! Toma tiempo de mí en otros asuntos politicos que son más importantes. Él es un puto idiota." (That shit governor is always bothering me with stupid issues! He takes time away from me and other political matters that are much more important. He's a fucking idiot.)

They approach an overpass and all hell breaks loose. A rocket propelled grenade slams into the lead car causing a violent explosion. On fire, it swerves to the right into a steep ditch. A massive deluge of bullets rain down on the second car, penetrating glass, metal, and human flesh. The hot shrapnel slices four state police officers into shreds. The mayor screams, "Qué carajo está pasando? Mueve el puto coche y vamos a la mierda de aquí." (What the fuck is going on? Move the fucking car and get the shit out of here.)

He lays flat on the floor of the backseat and can feel his heart beat like a war drum. He can smell blood in his nostrils and the explosions are ear shattering. Projectiles now find his car and tear through the windshield killing everyone except him. Silence now engulfs the air. He peeks out the window and sees the four escort state police cars on fire and peppered with bullet holes. Black smoke covers the area. He slowly lies back down on the floor trying desperately to disappear. Seconds seem like hours and then he hears voices. The door of his car abruptly flies open and two men quickly grab his ankles and drag him out slamming him violently onto the ground. He sees several armed men frowning at him.

He says, "Sabes quién soy? Soy el alcalde de Juárez!" (Do you know who I am? I'm the mayor of Juarez!)

One of the sicarios looks down on him, "Alcalde, usted no es alcalde! Usted es un protector del Cartel del Norte, pinche cabrón." (Mayor, you are no mayor! You are a protector of the Cartel of the North, fucking bastard.)

The sicario yells, "Dame la gasolina! Date prisa, no tenemos todo el día. El resto de ustedes cargen el camión con los muertos." (Give me the gasoline! Hurry, we don't have all day. The rest of you load the truck with the dead.) The sicario pours the gasoline on the mayor as he cries and begs for his life. A match is lit and thrown on the mayor who is immediately engulfed in scorching flames. He jumps to his feet and runs a few feet as his lungs fill with suffocating fire and his eyeballs begin to boil and then violently explode out of their sockets. He falls and his body is incinerated in minutes. The sicarios take the rest of the corpses to the nearby overpass and tie their feet with rope and then throw them over the side. The bodies sway back and forth bumping into one another in a morbid dance. Two sicarios hang a narco message above the corpses. It reads:

ESTOS SON LOS PERROS QUE PROTEGEN EL CARTEL DEL NORTE. TODOS QUE ESTÁN EN LA CAMA CON ALBINO ROMERO VA A CORRER LA MISMA SUERTE.

(These are the dogs that protect the Cartel of the North. Everyone who is in bed with Albino Romero will suffer the same fate.)

The savage war between cartels escalates, making the conflict between Afghanistan and Iraq look like a shouting match between two junior high kids. The bodies began to pile up and it becomes dangerous for the army of sicarios belonging to Atenco to dump them on the sides of roads, rivers and ravines. Patrols by the military and police increase and they capture several sicarios getting rid of cadavers. To deal with the problem, La Sombra calls a friend of his, Pedro Amaya, who is a pozolero (A stewmaker) to help them. Amaya is a short, thin man with coarse hair and a large scar running down his left cheek. It is a reminder of a fight at a brothel over a young prostitute. Amaya shot and killed the young soldier, but not before getting stabbed several times.

He wears the scar on his face as a badge of honor. His machismo was the only thing that mattered to him.

Amaya is honored to help his old friend and agrees to work out of Chihuahua where the conflict is in full swing. Amaya is able to find an old house twenty miles south of Juarez. Conveniently, it is off the beaten path. He drives his truck to Juarez and purchases several used metal fifty-five gallon barrels and several hundred pounds of caustic soda (Sodium hydroxide). He pays a dollar fifty for each pound of the caustic soda. Amaya also buys a large box of latex gloves and gas masks. He is ready to make his first batch of pozole. It is a traditional Mexican stew consisting of hominy, pork and chili. Amaya has his own special recipe for pozole, but instead of pork, he uses human flesh.

Two days later, Amaya receives a call from one of the sicarios who tells him they have four bodies that need to disappear. He meets up with them at a shopping center parking lot in downtown Juarez and they trade cars. Amaya then drives the black Hyundai SUV with the four bodies back to his house. He brings his two sons, Antonio and Geronimo, to help him with his gruesome work. They are psychopaths, just like their father. They begin their work and stuff each body in a barrel and then fill the metal containers halfway with water. Next, they add several pounds of caustic soda. They start a fire underneath each barrel using chopped wood and soon the water begins to boil. The caustic soda begins to breakdown the chemical bonds that keep the flesh intact. Within twenty-four hours, the bodies turn into liquid with a coffee like appearance. Amaya looks into the barrels and sees the only solid material that remains are bone hulls that can now be easily crushed even with one's fingers. Amaya's sons take the barrels and dump the contents into a pit they

196 Michael S. Vigil

dug and then pour gasoline into it. The intense fire destroys the last remnants of evidence.

Within six months, the pozolero dissolves more than four hundred bodies, all of them men. He doesn't know who they are and quite frankly, it is not important to him. He is paid seven thousand dollars each month, plus a stipend for the materials used in his disposal business. Amaya buys hundreds of pounds of caustic soda every week from a local hardware store. Eventually, a woman who is a cashier asks why he buys so much of the acid. He tells her that he owns a cleaning business and uses it to clean houses. She frowns, but accepts his story.

Amaya is exhausted from his work, which is now twenty-four hours a day. He buys more barrels and more acid, but he is unable to dissolve all the bodies the cartel gives him. He now starts to pile them in an old storage shed behind the house. With the hot temperatures, they start to decompose and the stench is unbearable. He decides to hire five of his cousins to help him and asks La Sombra for more money.

He tells him, "Señor, estoy trabajando como un perro y tratando de mantener con la demanda de pozole. Es difícil y necesito que mis primos vengan y me ayudan. Es por esta razón que voy a necesitar más dinero para pagarlos. Sus hombres están haciendo su trabajo y me dan más carne de cerdo que necesito para mi pozole, pero necesitan de su apoyo financiero." (Sir, I'm working like a dog and trying to keep up with the demand for pozole. It is difficult and need for my cousin's to come and help me. It is for this reason that I will need more money to pay them. Your men are doing their job and provide me with more pork than I need for my pozole, but I need your financial support.)

La Sombra says, "No es problema, te pagaré cinquenta mil al mes y que debería cubrir el salario de ellos. Estas haciendo un buen trabajo. Vamos a enviar más carne de cerdo en el próximo par de meses. Es necesario para abastecerse de suministros y te va a enviar dinero para comprarlos." (Not a problem, I'll pay you fifty thousand per month and that should cover their salaries. You're doing a good job. We will send more pork to you in the next couple of months. You need to stock up on supplies and I will send money to buy them.)

"Gracias! Me ayudará a seguir con mi trabajo. Espero que estés bien y está de buen humor. Usted sabe que siempre puede confiar en mí. Hago mi trabajo mejor que nadie." (Thank you! It will help me to continue my work. I hope you are well and in good spirits. You know that you can always trust me. I do my job better than anyone.)

The next day, Amaya goes to a car dealership and sees the perfect vehicle he needs for his gruesome business. It is a used meat truck with refrigeration. He pays cash and one of his sons drives it from the parking lot. Amaya smiles and starts to whistle. He is happy. He has found the perfect solution for storing the rising number of bodies, which he has to quickly make into pozole. The side of the truck bears an old business logo that is quite ironic,

LAS CARNES PARA EL GUSTO MÁS REFINADO.

(Meats for the most refined taste.)

Amaya howls with a sinister laugh. It is business as usual and he looks forward to possibly offering his skills to other cartels.

Villa is at home one evening watching CNN Latino and gets a phone call from Ventura who says that Rafael, a/k/a

La Serpiente, has been killed in Los Mochis, Sinaloa. Apparently, he snuck back into Mexico to secretly hookup with his girlfriend and was killed by gunmen belonging to the Cartel of the North. While he was at a seafood restaurant with the girl, two men with AR-15s stormed in and fired several rounds killing both of them instantly. After hanging up, Villa remembers his dream in Juarez about a vulture looking down at a dead snake. He is convinced it was a premonition that Rafael was going to die.

The war continues in Juarez with a horrific death toll. One evening, Atenco's sicarios follow two known members of the Cartel of the North into the downtown area. They watch as their rival's white Lexus slows as it enters a dark residential street and finally stops in front of a red brick house.

Using the element of surprise, the sicarios leap from the car and yell, "Manos arriba, hijos de puta! No se muevan." (Hands up, sons of whores! Do not move.)

One of the men goes for his gun tucked in his pants, but the front sight snags on the waistband. The sicarios fire their weapons striking him three times in the chest and once in his face. The .45 caliber slug enters his left eye and tears through the brain ripping off half of his skull. Gray matter flows through the gaping wound.

The other man screams, "No me mates! No me mates!" (Don't kill me! Don't kill me!)

The sicarios tell him, "Rápidamente, tira el arma en el suelo! Puto perro, vas a venir con nosotros." (Quickly, throw your gun on the ground! Fucking dog, you're coming with us.) The fat man with rosy cheeks, wearing cowboy boots and a Dodgers baseball hat, slowly pulls his .9mm pistol from the small of his back and throws it on the ground. He is hit on the head with a pistol and blood streaks across his face. The sicarios throw him into the back seat of their car and drive away. Everyone is silent until they arrive at one of the sicarios' hideouts.

They pull the fat man out and shove him face first on the ground. He groans in pain. They drag him over into a shack and tie him to a chair. One of the sicarios punches him in the face knocking out several front teeth.

He grabs him by the hair, pulls his face close into his and says, "Hijo de puta! Dónde podemos encontrar a Lisa y otros amigos suyos? Si no nos dice lo que queremos saber, que va a morir una muerte miserable. Dinos-- quen protege el Cartel del Norte y donde se oculta el dinero y las drogas?" (Son of a whore! Where can we find Lisa and your other friends? If you do not tell us what we want to know, you will die a miserable death. Tell us-- who protects the Cartel of the North and where is their money and drugs hidden?)

"Por favor, no sé lo que está hablando. No sé de ningún cártel, dinero o drogas. Yo trabajo en la construcción. Yo tengo una familia. Por favor, no me hagas daño." (Please, I do not know what you're talking about. I do not know of any cartel, money or drugs. I work in construction. I have a family. Please do not hurt me.)

The sicario hits him with a lead pipe and screams at him, "Los próximos golpes, idiota, estarán en su puta cabeza. Te mataré! Usted dice que trabaja en la construcción y llevar un arma? Usted debe pensar que somos estúpidos." (The next blows, idiot, will be on your fucking head. I'll kill you! You say you work in construction and you carry a gun? You must think we're stupid.)

"De acuerdo, te diré todo lo que sé. No trabajo transportando drogas o dinero y rara vez miro a Lisa. Yo garantizo la seguridad de algunos de los jefes de plaza cuando me llaman. Voy a contarles acerca de un Senador EE.UU. de Texas que protege el cartel. Su nombre es Simón García y él es un hombre poderoso. Él proporciona el cartel con información sobre las investigaciones y operaciones. Se reúne regularmente con las agencias de Estados Unidos para obtener informados y luego pasa la información al cartel. Se le paga millones de dólares cada año. He estado allí cuando maletas de dinero se dan a él. El visita el Consulado EE.UU. en Juárez cada semana y aprovecha la ocasión para pasar información valiosa a nosotros." (Okay, I'll tell you everything I know. I don't work transporting drugs or money and rarely see Lisa. I guarantee the security of some of the plaza bosses when they call me. I'll tell you about a U.S. senator from Texas that protects the cartel. His name is Simon Garcia and he is a powerful man. He provides the cartel with information on investigations and operations. He meets regularly with U.S. law enforcement and intelligence agencies to get briefings and then passes the information to the cartel. He is paid several million dollars each year. I've been there when suitcases of money are given to him. He visits the U.S. Consulate in Juarez each week and takes the opportunity to give us valuable information.)

The sicario asks, "Como se mira y qué carro conduce? Visita el consulado en un día específico? Qué seguridad tiene cuando viene a Juárez? (What does he look like and what car does he drive? Does he visit the consulate on a specific day? What kind of security does he have when he comes to Juarez?)

"Es un hombre alto y delgado, con el pelo oscuro. Él es de tez oscura y tiene una nariz demasiado grande para su cara. Se le puede google. Él tiene un sitio web con su foto. Viene a Juárez el viernes por la tarde para que pueda obtener su dinero después de que visita el consulado. Conduce un Mercedes-Benz negro con placas de Texas. Viene solo para que nadie lo verá reunirse con nosotros." (He is a tall, thin man with dark hair. He is of dark complexion and has a nose too big for his face. You can google him. He has a website with his photo and background on it. He comes to Juarez on Friday afternoon so he can get his money after visiting the consulate. He drives a black Mercedes Benz with Texas plates. He comes by himself so no one will see him meet with us.)

The sicario, after getting the information he wants, steps behind the bound prisoner and fires a single bullet into his right ear. Blood gushes from his head as he slumps forward in the chair.

The sicario says, "Hijo de puta, puso sangre en mis botas nuevas! Yo debería matarlo otra vez." (Motherfucker, he got blood on my new boots. I should kill him again.) Both sicarios fall to their knees in laughter.

La Sombra receives a call from the sicarios in Juarez. They tell him about the senator who allegedly helps the Cartel of the North. He listens carefully as he knows that a decision will have to come directly from him. He has to be sure it is the correct one.

They ask, "Qué quieres que hagamos? (What you want us to do?)

La Sombra tells them, "Mátalo! Sólo asegúrese de que no se encuentra un solo pelo de el. Tienes que hacer desaparecer su coche. Ni rastro debe ser encontrado de el." (Kill him! Just make sure that not a single hair of his is found. You have to make his car disappear. No trace is to remain of him.)

Early the next Friday, six sicarios arrive at the U.S. Consulate in two cars with tinted windows and park across the busy street. They eat warm tortas with thick slices of fresh avocado and wait for their prey. Some of them nap while others watch as cars arrive at the diplomatic post. Finally, just past noon a black Mercedes-Benz with Texas tags arrives and parks in front. They see the senator get out of his car wearing a blue pinstripe suit with a flashy, yellow tie. He enters the building. The sicarios notice he is alone. No more than an hour passes before the senator struts out the front door. He seems completely oblivious to his surroundings as he enters his luxury late model sedan. He drives away slowly and is easily followed to an abandoned factory south of the city. He parks and waits patiently. The sicarios don't want to wait and they attack. At gunpoint they force the senator into one of their cars and two of them get into his car and drive away.

The terrified senator protests, "Qué diablos está pasando! Sabes quién soy? Usted me debe liberar inmediatamente." (What the hell is going on? Do you know who I am? You must release me immediately.)

One of the sicarios smashes the butt of his pistol to the side of his head and says, "Cállate! No nos importa lo que eres. Todo lo que sabemos es que ayuda a los perros putos del Cartel del Norte. No digas una palabra o te mataré." (Shut up! We don't care who you are. All we know is that you help the fucking dogs of the Cartel of the North. Don't say another word or I'll kill you.)

The sicarios drive the Senator who is dripping wet from perspiration to where the pozolero lives. The others drive the senator's car to the desert where they have already dug a huge pit. They park on the lip of the hole and get out of the vehicle. One of the sicarios presses the accelerator with his hand then quickly backs away. The car pitches forward and pitches into the pit with a resounding crash. It takes hours, but the car is finally buried under several feet of dirt and no one will ever find it. Meantime, the pozolero is now eyeing the senator like a choice piece of meat for his next stew. The sicarios tie the Senator's hands behind his back and also his legs. They place a plastic bag over his head and wrap it tightly with duct tape around his neck. He breathes hard and the little oxygen in the bag is quickly consumed. As he slowly suffocates, the senator struggles violently, but the bindings hold and he knows that death is imminent. He gasps loudly as he takes his last breath. His head rolls to his left and his eyes can be seen through the clear plastic. They are wide open and severely bloodshot.

A sicario tells Amaya, "Esta es una prioridad! Es necesario disolver éste ahora mismo. Ni una sola uña de sus manos debe ser encontrado. Lo entiendes? (This is a priority! It is necessary to dissolve this one now. Not a single nail from his hands should be found. You understand?)

"Por supuesto! Voy a empezar ahora. Él será sólo un recuerdo en unas pocas horas. Nada quedará de él." (Of course! I'll start now. He will be just a memory in a few hours. Nothing will be left of him.)

Amaya and his crew lift the dead senator and dump him head first into one of the barrels. Quickly, they fill it with water from a garden hose. Then they add the caustic soda and light a fire to bring it to a boil. Soon bubbles can be seen coming to the surface. Despite the gas masks, Amaya can feel the fumes aggravating his throat and lungs. Within hours, the body starts to disintegrate and shrink down further in the barrel. Less than a day later, nothing remains of the illustrious senator. A lifetime is erased in a few hours.

One of Amaya's younger cousins, Santiago, is psychologically coming apart. He can no longer endure the violence and depravity. His Catholic conscience rebels at what they are doing to the dead bodies. He is positive that he is going straight to hell for dissolving God's creations. One day he goes into Juarez and finds a pay phone. He calls the DEA office in Mexico City and talks to Villa.

Santiago tells him, "Señor, mi nombre es Santiago y ha estado trabajando con mi primo cerca de Juárez. Él es un pozolero y hemos ido disolviendo cientos de cadáveres asesinados por sicarios del Cartel Alianza de Sangre. Me siento enfermo de culpabilidad y sé que Dios me va a castigar." (Sir, my name is Santiago and I have been working with my cousin near Juarez. He is a pozolero and we have been dissolving hundreds of corpses killed by hitmen from the Blood Alliance Cartel. I feel sick with guilt and I know God is going to punish me.)

Villa says, "Estoy seguro de que Dios te perdonará si me das todo lo que sabes. Cuál es el nombre de su primo y donde están haciendo la disolución de los cuerpos?" (I am sure that God will forgive you if you tell me everything you know. What is the name of your cousin and where is he dissolving the bodies?")

"Si señor, su nombre es Pedro Amaya y la casa es de unos treinta kilómetros al sur de Juárez en la Carretera 11. Hay un enorme árbol al lado de la carretera y una vieja pared hecha de roca en la entrada. Es fácil de encontrar." (Yes sir, his name is Pedro Amaya and the house is about thirty kilometers south of Juarez on road 11. There is a huge tree beside the road and an old wall made of rock at the entrance. It is easy to find.)

Villa tells him, "Agradezco la información. No regrese al rancho. Debe abandonar la zona. Voy a tomar de este asunto inmediatamente." (I appreciate the information. Do not return to the ranch. You must leave the area. I will take care of this matter immediately.)

Villa calls Ventura and gives him the information. Ventura has heard of the pozolero, but had never identified him. He thanks Villa and then calls his men who are in Juarez. Within three hours a convoy of three black sedans is speeding up the road to the pozolero's house. They quickly find the house and see several large barrels scattered out in front. The cars skid to a screeching halt. The Mexican agents charge out and kick down the front door. Amaya and his cousins are shit faced on tequila and in the process of cooking a huge cauldron of seafood stew. They are handcuffed by the agents and put down hard on the ground. Amaya tries to speak, but the only thing that comes out his mouth is saliva, which drips down his chin. In the back of the house they find fifty bodies in the meat truck, large amounts of caustic soda, barrels and gas masks. Amaya admits to being a pozolero and dissolving over a thousand men. He never mentions the senator.

A year later, the U.S. Congress holds a memorial service for the senator. They honor his integrity, service, and patriotism. They also commemorate his heroic commitment in fighting the scourge of illegal drugs.

CHAPTER
10

The Escape

Romero reclines on a bed made of poured concrete and a disgusting and filthy one-inch thick mattress. His new domain consists of a cell, eight by twelve feet in Mexico's most secure prison- *La Palma*.

Located ten kilometers south of Mexico City, it is home to some of the most dangerous criminals on earth. All of Mexico's drug lords are incarcerated here. It is the Who's Who of the drug trade. No one has ever escaped from this prison despite many attempts that have proved futile. When transferred to the facility, Romero saw hardened and ruthless men breakdown and cry because it was essentially the end of the line for them. It took two years to build the prison and the Mexican government didn't spare any expense in making it virtually escape proof. After the construction was complete, the American Corrections Association did an audit and certified La Palma in the areas of safety, security, order, care, programs, justice, and administration. It was certified in everything except the human factor, the most critical key to security. It was one of the first prisons in the country to receive certification, but immense wealth and power can overcome high walls and steel bars.

Romero looks around his cell and focuses on a twelve-inch black and white television that has the same dumb and boring shows, including closed circuit educational classes and a religious programming lineup of pure hell that are repeated over and over again. He has a four-inch wide window to look out into the prisons' inner courtyard. It is this compressed view of the world that allows him to maintain his sanity. Romero has a small, immovable concrete desk and stool. His toilet, sink, and water fountain are combined into one unit. He also has a shower that is on a timer to prevent potential flooding. The food is barely fit for human consumption. Not even the stray mongrel dogs that roam the streets would touch it.

Within days of his arrival at the prison, Romero begins to spread large amounts of money to the prison guards. They quickly refer to him as *El Jefe*. He pays the guards to buy food for him daily from the best restaurants in the city. He has hundreds of menus from different ethnic restaurants in his cell. Early each morning, one of the guards takes his order for lunch and dinner. The food is picked up and delivered hot to his cell. A bottle of expensive wine accompanies each meal. Prison is hell.

Romero is visited by some of Mexico's most beautiful women and he is given a private area for his almost daily sexual encounters. He orders hundreds of Viagra tablets each month and several pharmacies are told to have large reserves for *El Jefe*. He has everything money can buy except his freedom. He has a lot of time to plot and plan while he sits alone in his cell. Romero is one of the most intelligent criminal masterminds of his time and solitude is a dangerous thing for someone of his genius.

His primary attorney, Juan Fernandez, visits him early one day and tells him of all the *amparos* (legal injunctions) that have been filed on his behalf to stop his extradition to the U.S. Fernandez tells him that eight different U.S. federal jurisdictions are going to request his extradition.

He says, "Albino, usted tiene que saber que si eres extraditado, es el final para usted. Te van a enterrar con cargos criminales. Es por eso que necesitamos luchar contra esta situación. Vamos a luchar legalmente, pero hay que hacerlo con todo su red criminal también." (Albino, you have to know that if you are extradited, it is the end for you. They will bury you with criminal charges. You will never see daylight again. That's why we need to fight this situation. We will fight legally, but you must also do it with your criminal network as well.)

"Sí, Juan! Entiendo la situación. Usted y mis otros abogados tienen que presentar amparos con el fin de darme tiempo. Me has traído el teléfono celular que te pedí?" (Yes, Juan! I understand the situation. You and my other lawyers have to keep submitting injunctions in order to give me time. Did you bring the cell phone I asked for?) Fernandez says, "Sí, aquí está el teléfono celular y el cargador. Usted sabe que está en contra de la reglas de la prisión, pero estoy seguro de que ya se ha encargado de eso. Que más necesitas?" (Yes, here is the cell phone and charger. You know it is against the regulations of the prison, but I'm sure you've already taken care of that. What else do you need?)

"Quiero que le digas a David Naranjo, quien construye mis túneles de drogas a los EE.UU. que venga a verme inmediatamente. Ahora que tengo un teléfono, me encuentro en una situación mucho mejor." (I want you to tell David Naranjo, who builds my drug tunnels into the U.S., to come see me immediately. Now that I have a phone, I'm in a much better situation.)

The very next day, Naranjo shows up at the prison and is pissed off because of all the search and control areas he has to go through. He is mistaken for an American because of his blonde hair and blue eyes. He is tall and gaunt with a world class attitude. Naranjo is a graduate of the prestigious German Clausthal University of Technology where he earned a degree in underground mining technology and machinery. He was immediately recruited after he returned to Mexico by the Cartel of the North to build tunnels that were used to smuggle tons of drugs into the U.S. He has built hundreds of them, literally making the Mexico/U.S. border a virtual block of Swiss cheese. After a short wait, Romero strolls in and gives Naranjo a hug.

Romero tells him, "David, es bueno verte! Cómo está tu familia? Gracias por venir a verme tan rápidamente." (David, good to see you! How is your family? Thanks for coming to see me so quickly.)

"Albino, es bueno verte también. Mi familia está haciendo bien, gracias por preguntar. Esta prisión es jodidamente horrible. Tiene tanta seguridad." (Albino, good to see you too. My family is doing well, thanks for asking. This prison is fucking horrible. They have so much security.) Albino whispers, "Escucha con atención, mis abogados me han dicho que los EE.UU. pronto van a pedir mi extradición. Si eso sucede, voy a morir en un país extranjero. Joder los gringos, moriré antes de ir allí. Es necesario utilizar sus habilidades para construir un túnel de escape para mí." (Listen attentively, my lawyers have told me the U.S. will soon ask for my extradition. If that happens, I will tragically die in a foreign country. Fuck the Americans, I will die before I go there. You must use your skills to build an escape tunnel for me.)

Naranjo frowns, "Tienes que estar bromeando! Sabes está prisión es la mas segura en el pais. Tienen las patrullas de seguridad alrededor de la prisión y la zona residencial más cercana es más de tres kilometros de distancia. Es casi imposible." (You've got to be kidding! You know this prison is the most secure in the country. They have security patrols around the prison and the nearest residential area is more than three kilometers away. It's almost impossible.)

Romero laughs, "Mi amigo, nada es imposible! Yo sé que el túnel va a ser muy largo, pero sé que puede hacerlo. Es necesario comenzar a planificar y empezar a trabajar rápidamente. El dinero no es problema y usted será un hombre muy rico." (My friend, nothing is impossible! I know that the tunnel will be very long, but I know you can do it. You need to start planning and working quickly. Money is no problem and you will be a very rich man.)

"Albino, lo haré para usted! Voy a encontrar una casa que está un poco aislado o puede que tenga que comprar un pedazo de la propiedad y construir una estructura superficial para ocultar la excavación del túnel. También tendrá que

212 Michael S. Vigil

darme dinero para el equipo y algunos de mis trabajadores de confianza. Por cierto, tienes que conseguirme los planos de la prisión. Esto es muy crítico." (Albino, I'll do it for you! I'll find a house that is a bit isolated or we may have to buy a piece of property and build a rustic structure to hide the tunnel excavation. You also need to give me money for equipment and to pay some of my most trusted employees. By the way, you have to get me the blueprints of the prison. This is very critical.)

Albino responds, "Mi abogado, Fernández, les dará todo lo que necesita. Voy a conseguir los planos a la prisión. Tenemos que actuar con rapidez. Voy a pagar a los guardias o los amenazo, si es necesario. De cualquier manera, van a cooperar." (My lawyer, Fernandez, will give you whatever you need. I'll get the blueprints to the prison. We need to act quickly. I will pay the guards or threaten them, if necessary. Either way, they will cooperate.)

Naranjo leaves the prison and knows he is expected to build the most complex narco tunnel the world has ever seen. Truthfully, though he protested, he knows he will make history by building the most sophisticated prison escape tunnel. He will be famous. Standing in front of the prison, he scans the area in the distance. He sees a poor cinder block home a hundred yards away from the poor village nearby and about three kilometers from La Palma. He will be off to a good start, if he can buy the fucking house. He walks at a brisk pace and gets into his cherry red Lexus RC convertible. Naranjo takes a narrow dirt road and navigates the deep potholes and large rocks. Cursing, he arrives at the house and sees a man in tattered clothing watering a small garden of tomatoes.

He yells from the car, "Oye, eres el propietario de esta casa? (Hey, are you the owner of this house?)

The gray haired, wrinkled old man wearing old huaraches looks up and curiously looks first at the fancy car and then at Naranjo. He is perplexed and thinks the man must be lost.

He answers, "Sí señor, yo soy el dueño. He estado viviendo aquí por cinco años." (Yes sir, I am the owner. I've been living here for five years.)

Naranjo says, "Está interesado en vender su lugar? El hijo de mi hermana está encarcelado en La Palma y es difícil que viaje constantemente de Nogales, Sonora, para verlo. Ella quiere estar cerca de la prisión donde ella puede visitar todos los días. Ya sabes cómo son las madres." (Are you interested in selling your place? My sister's son is imprisoned in La Palma and it is difficult for her to constantly travel from Nogales, Sonora, to see him. She wants to be near the prison where she can visit him every day. You know how mothers are.)

"Si señor, entiendo cómo una madre quiere estar cerca de su hijo. Soy de Chiapas y, a decir verdad, me gustaría volver allí. Pero tendría que conseguir un buen precio. Sé que es una casa pobre, pero su hermana sería cómodo." (Yes sir, I understand how a mother wants to be near her son. I'm from Chiapas and, truth be told, I'd like to go back there. But I would have to get a good price. I know it's a poor house, but your sister would be comfortable.)

Naranjo asks, "Pues déjeme preguntarle, cuánto pago por ella?" (Well let me ask, how much did you pay for it?)

"Compré la casa y la propiedad por doscientos mil pesos. Aún debo la mitad y he estado teniendo un tiempo difícil ya que sólo ha conseguir trabajo temporalmente como obrero." (I bought the house and property for two hundred thousand pesos. I still owe half of it and I've been having a hard time because I am only able to get part time work as a laborer.)

Naranjo smiles, "Bueno, te pagaré un millón de pesos y pago lo que debe en la casa. Hay una condición, que me de la casa en los próximos dos días. Voy a tener que remodelar para mi hermana. Tenemos un trato?" (Well, I will pay you a million pesos and pay what you owe on the house. There is a condition, you have to give me the house in the next two days. I'll have to remodel it for my sister. Do we have a deal?)

"Por supuesto, tenemos un trato. Puede hacer lo que quiera con las pocas piezas de muebles que tengo o los puede tirar a la basura. Tan pronto como me pagas, puedes tener la casa. Dios me ha bendecido. Gracias Señor." (Of course, we have a deal. You can keep the few pieces of furniture I have or you can throw them in the trash. As soon as you pay me, you can have the house. God has blessed me. Thank you, sir.)

Naranjo is pleased it went so well and quick. Now he has to get some of his tunnel rats together and buy the equipment to start building the tunnel of tunnels. He knows Romero will be happy things are starting to fall into place.

The pollution in Mexico City is overpowering and Ricardo Martinez, warden of La Palma, walks into a small restaurant in the downtown area to have a bowl of tortilla soup. His eyes are burning and his throat is sore from sucking in high levels of caustic vapors. Martinez is a strongly built man with curly brown hair. He is dressed in a conservative three-piece brown suit and a matching brown striped tie. He looks more like a businessman than a warden. As always, he is in a bad mood because he hates his job. He joined Mex-

ico's most powerful political party, the Partido Revolu-
cionario Institucional (PRI), as a teenager hoping to land a
prestigious and well-paid job. Things didn't work out as he
planned. He was promptly told that he served the needs of
the party and should be glad to be in charge of La Palma. He
hates to deal with low life criminals who complain about
everything and threaten him constantly. He has reoccurring
dreams of torching the entire prison and everything in it. His
health is getting progressively worse and he suffers from
high blood pressure, insomnia, and bleeding ulcers cause
him unbearable pain every fucking day. As he begins to eat
his soup, two nasty looking men in dark shirts and pants approach his table and sit down.

Martinez asks them, "Señores, puedo ayudarles en algo?"
(Gentlemen, can I help you with something?)

The men stare menacingly at Martinez, like two hungry
wolves about to devour a fawn. Finally, one of them speaks
as Martinez breaks out in a cold sweat. He says, "Escucha,
porque no voy a repetirme. Tenemos un proyecto y necesitamos su ayuda. Estamos dispuestos a pagar mucho dinero
por sus servicios. Mucho más de lo que se le paga trabajando
para el gobierno en cincuenta años." (Listen, because I will
not repeat myself. We have a project and need your help. We
are willing to pay a lot of money for your services. Much
more than what you would be paid working for the government in fifty years.)

Martinez replies, "Quien diablos son ustedes? Qué tipo
de servicio estas hablando? Ni siquiera sé quenes son y por
qué me están ofreciendo dinero." (Who the hell are you?
What kind of service are you talking about? I do not even
know who you are or why you are offering me money.)

The man with the gold-capped teeth looks at Martinez like he would like nothing better then to snuff him out. In a strong voice, he says, "Queremos los planos de La Palma. Esto no es un juego que estamos jugando contigo, idiota. Los planos serán entregados a nosotros mañana. Ni siquiera piences en llamar a la policía." (We want the blueprints to La Palma. This is not a game we're playing with you, idiot. The blueprints will be delivered to us tomorrow. Don't even think about calling the police.)

Martinez feels a migraine coming on and his blood pressure is about to cause his arteries to explode as if they were cheap garden hoses. He is overcome with nausea since he knows that he is in the presence of pure evil. One of the men pulls something out of his pocket and throws color photos of his wife and two daughters on top of the table.

He tells Martinez, "Si usted no entrega los planos mañana, vamos a matar a su esposa, hijas, y luego vamos a desmembrar a usted mientras usted todavía está vivo. Sea inteligente y tomar el dinero. Usted sólo tiene dos opciones y tomar el dinero es la mejor. Dime ahora lo que quiere hacer." (If you do not deliver the blueprints tomorrow, we will kill your wife, daughters, and then we'll dismember you while you are still alive. Be smart and take the money. You only have two options and taking the money is the best. Tell me now what you want to do.)

Martinez is about to pass out, but tries to hold it together. Now he is even more pissed at the PRI for putting him in this predicament. Taking the job as warden and dealing with men who hold nothing sacred is the worst decision he has ever made.

Finally, he says, "Bueno, voy a conseguir los planos para mañana. Por favor, no hagan daño a mi familia. Hare lo que quieras." (Okay, I'll get the blueprints for you tomorrow. Please do not hurt my family. I will do what you want.)

Martinez stumbles out of the restaurant and his mind is racing a thousand miles an hour. He is concerned and knows that he is between a rock and a hard spot. But in the end, he decides it is better to end up in jail then lose his life and the lives of the people he loves most in the world.

Little does Martinez know that several of his guards and the staff of the prison command and control center are also being approached and offered a choice, take the money or face a brutal death. They are not told anything other than they will be called upon to do a service in the near future. All decide to take the bribes, some because they are corrupt and others because they are afraid of being killed.

In less than a week, Naranjo begins construction of the tunnel. He uses generators for power, jackhammers, winches to remove displaced earth, and a micro-tunneling machine that can bore through hard packed dirt and rock. Picks and shovels are used to widen the tunnel. The house he bought allows them to hide their activities as they continue moving underground towards the forbidding prison. Naranjo calculates a distance of five thousand two hundred and eighty feet from the house to Romero's cell. He figures they can dig about fifteen feet a day and it will take about three hundred and fifty-two days to finish the tunnel. He uses fifteen of his most seasoned tunnel diggers. They are used to hard labor and are highly motivated by the money Romero will pay them. Naranjo mathematically estimates having to remove two thousand seven hundred tons of dirt. It is a massive undertaking. It will take at least four hundred truckloads. He comes up with an ingenious idea. He will buy a couple of used dump trucks and then spread the word in the nearby village that the new owners of the cinder block house work at construction sites transporting gravel. The trucks will be loaded with dirt at night and each morning leave for an isolated area ten miles from the prison where they will dump it.

The blueprints to La Palma provided by Martinez are vital to Naranjo. He can now excavate safely and avoid water and power lines. The blueprints also show the spacing of the rebar reinforcing the concrete on the ground level of the prison. He uses this information to find the proper tool that will be used to punch a hole into the prison when the time comes. More importantly, Naranjo now pinpoints the exact location of Romero's cell since global positioning systems don't work underground. He knows that the most important factor in building a tunnel is that it fits the purpose for which it is designed. It will be rustic since the ultimate objective of the excavation is to facilitate an escape. Naranjo makes sure that the tunnel follows the designated route with precise, absolute coordinates. He is expert at translating complex design data into a finished tunnel and relies on the use of sophisticated surveying equipment, which is a challenge due to the confined spaces and underground environment. Naranjo relies on *Total Stations*, the primary instrument used in mining surveying. The total stations measure and record positions with precision.

Naranjo goes down to thirty feet below the surface and finally hits thick clay. *Perfect*, he thinks. It will prevent the tunnel from collapsing and will only need minimal support infrastructure. Oxygen is pumped in as the tunnel begins to get longer. PVC pipe is put in the tunnel and a large air pump pushes oxygen through the pipes and keeps it well ventilated.

Fernandez, the attorney, visits Romero to deliver the status of the tunnel. Quietly, he whispers, "El proyecto va bien, pero va a estar cerca de un año antes de que te alcance. Usted tendrá que mantener la calma y ser paciente. Empezar a pensar en su plan una vez que escapar y salir por el otro extremo del túnel. También debe saber que el túnel va a costar más de cinco millones de dólares." (The project is going well, but it will be about a year before it will reach you. You have to stay calm and be patient. Start thinking about your plan once you escape and come out the other end of the tunnel. You should also know that the tunnel will cost more than five million dollars.)

"Yo sé que el túnel llevará tiempo. Mientras tanto, mantenga el sistema judicial ocupado con amparos para evitar mi extradición. Cuando salgo de este miserable lugar, voy a tomar un avión a Colombia y estará bajo la protección de mis amigos en la FARC. No se preocupe por el dinero, hago más de cinco millones de dólares en menos de diez horas." (I know the tunnel will take time. Meanwhile, keep the justice system busy with injunctions to prevent my extradition. When I leave this miserable place, I'll take a plane to Colombia and will be under the protection of my friends in the FARC. Do not worry about money, I make more than five million dollars in less then ten hours.)

In Sinaloa, Atenco is in a murderous rage. Things are not going well and his drug operations are being disrupted by the war against the Cartel of the North and law enforcement. He calls for La Sombra who walks in and knows what is coming.

Atenco tells him, "Debemos ejercer nuestro poder y enviar el mensaje a la puta de la DEA. Me han dicho que es un agente de la DEA con el nombre de Villa que nos ha estado causando problemas. El trabaja en estrecha colaboración con un agente Mexicano con el nombre de Ventura que es su amigo. Usted va a matar a los dos. No podemos trabajar con ellos mordiendo nuestros talones como perros." (We must exercise our power and send a message to the fucking DEA. I'm told it's a DEA agent by the name of Villa who has been causing us problems. He is works in close collaboration with a Mexican agent by the name of Ventura who is his friend. You will kill them both. We cannot work with them biting at our heels like dogs.)

"Jefe, si matamos a un agente de la DEA, el gobierno de EE.UU. vendrá para nosotros con una venganza. Nos van a cazar en la tierra y en el cielo hasta que nos encuentren. Yo cumplo con sus órdenes, pero estás listo para enfrentar las consecuencias." (Boss, if we kill a DEA agent, the U.S. government will come for us with a vengeance. They will hunt us on Earth and in heaven until they find us. I will comply with your orders, but are you ready to face the consequences?)

Atenco, quite irritated, says, "Si no hacemos nada, nadie nos va a respetar. Este negocio tiene que ver con el respeto. Sin eso, otros se roban de nosotros y apoderarse de nuestro territorio. El respeto y el miedo son las únicas dos cosas que las personas entienden. Quiero que mates a ellos tan pronto como sea posible." (If we do nothing, nobody will respect us. This business has to do with respect. Without it, others will steal from us and take over our territory. Respect and fear are the only two things that people understand. I want you to kill them as soon as possible.)

La Sombra bows his head, "A sus órdenes! No voy a necesitar más que un par de hombres, lo que permitirá que los sigamos discretamente hasta que encontremos el momento adecuado para ejecutarlos." (At your service! I will not take more than a couple of men allowing us to follow them discreetly until we find the right moment to execute them.)

Early the next day, La Sombra and two of his most vicious men leave for Mexico City. They drive through vibrant green agricultural fields with a slight tapestry of brightly colored flowers. They are in a good mood, but deep down La Sombra knows killing a DEA agent will come to no good.

Later that evening they arrive in Mexico City and check into the Nikko hotel about a mile from the U.S. Embassy. Once in his room, La Sombra gets on the Internet and researches Villa. He soon finds a newspaper article with a photo of him. The assassins go to bed early after having an early dinner of steak and lobster. They get wake up calls the next morning and are ready to start before normal working hours begin at the U.S. Embassy. They know embassy employees park their cars underneath the building or in a parking lot in the back. La Sombra, dressed in a cowboy hat and denim jeans is anxious to get started with his violent task. He wears sunglasses to hide his face. They park on the street behind the embassy and walk to the side door of the Maria Isabel Sheraton next to the embassy. They have a perfect view of the cars coming in and out of the diplomatic post. Less than an hour later, they see a dark sedan arrive and park in the back of the embassy. Suddenly, they see Villa emerge and walk to the back door of the building. La Sombra thinks it is best to kill Villa and Ventura at the same time. If done separately, it will be more difficult since the other target will become more security conscious and take extra precautions. They leave the area and return to the hotel where they plot strategy.

La Sombra thinks a few minutes and then says, "Esto es lo que vamos a hacer. Mañana, vamos a estacionar en la calle

222 Michael S. Vigil

que es la entrada al estacionamiento de la embajada. Cuando Villa sale, vamos a seguirlo a Ventura. Si los vemos juntos, los matamos. Hasta entonces, no hacemos nada." (This is what we will do. Tomorrow, we are going to park on the street close to the entrance of the embassy parking lot. When Villa leaves, we will follow him to Ventura. If we see them together, we'll kill them both at the same time. Until then, we do nothing.)

For the next three days, La Sombra and his men track Villa when he leaves the embassy. Sometimes in the heavy traffic and congested streets they lose him. They become frustrated, but are determined to finish the job. They begin to fantasize about killing Villa and Ventura and want to torture them for days before pumping bullets into the back of their heads.

On the fourth day, at noon, Villa leaves the embassy and is followed at a safe distance. La Sombra and his sicarios tail him to El Meson restaurant and see him go in. Fifteen minutes later, Ventura parks in front. As luck would have it, he is alone making it easier to kill him. He leaps up the brick stairs and quickly slides into the restaurant. La Sombra and his men salivate, much like predators in the wild just before a kill. They check their weapons and pull the slides back to chamber rounds into the breeches.

They wait five minutes and then La Sombra gives the order, "Vamos, el tiempo es ahora. Mantengan la calma y asegurarse de que están muertos. No vamos a tener una segunda oportunidad. No se preocupe de que nadie vea su cara. Serán tan asustado una vez que empiece el tiroteo que van a poner la cabeza hacia abajo." (Let's go, the time is now. Remain calm and make sure they are dead. We will not get a second chance. Do not worry about anyone seeing your face.

They will be so scared once the shooting starts they will put their heads down.)

The three assassins walk calmly towards the restaurant and dodge cars as they cross the busy street. Surprise is their greatest advantage. The only one whose blood pressure and heartbeat is normal is La Sombra's who has done this hundreds of times. As one of the assassins pulls his weapon and opens the door of the El Meson, a mother with three small boys bump into him causing him to lose his balance. As he stumbles to the floor a gunshot goes off with a loud startling boom from his weapon. La Sombra, moving quickly, trips over his man on the floor. Villa is sitting facing the door. He draws his weapon and kills the sicario on the floor. He then fires two rounds at La Sombra hitting him in the abdomen. Ventura shoots the third assassin, but La Sombra is not down yet and fires a single bullet hitting Villa in the leg. Two more thunderous explosions come from Villa's weapon, which almost seem simultaneous and two lethal projectiles hit La Sombra in the head splattering brain matter and blood on the wall. Amid the screams, patrons rush towards the door and some slide on the wet blood on the floor and fall on the dead assassins.

Villa is unaware he is wounded until he feels something hot and sticky running down his right leg. He then feels a dull throbbing pain. He grabs a cloth napkin from the table and applies pressure to stop the bleeding. Ventura walks over to the sicarios and determines that the Grim Reaper has greedily claimed their miserable souls. A minute later, the wail of sirens is heard in the distance and Villa continues to lose blood. He fights going into shock and lies still on the floor. The last thing he remembers were several people looking down at him in disbelief and concern.

Villa, later that afternoon, wakes up in a hospital room. A doctor, in an immaculate white coat, tells him that he is a very lucky man since the bullet didn't hit any bone and only nicked a major artery. Villa is groggy and asks if he can go home. He is not so lucky and will have to spend the night at the hospital for observation. Ventura and his men come to visit and tell him how blessed he is because the hospital is full of beautiful nurses. They all have a good laugh, but their laughs are forced and mirthless. They know how alarmingly close they came to losing him and their boss. They stay with Villa until he falls asleep. Ventura leaves five of his best men to protect his friend. The night is suddenly chilly.

The Mexican newspapers all carry stories on the death of La Sombra, the most famous and shadowy assassin in the history of Mexico. Most people have heard of the elusive criminal, but didn't really know if he was just legend or if he truly existed. In death, La Sombra becomes more famous than he was in life and is now of equal stature to Jesus Malverde.

La Sombra was laid to rest at Jardines de Humaya cemetery in Culiacan where all the major drug lords are buried. The celebrated drug traffickers are buried there in condominium like structures, replete with air conditioning, cable television, and running water. Some of the crypts cost half a million dollars. It is a cemetery for mainly young traffickers. Most are victims of violent deaths in the prime of their lives.

La Sombra is entombed in a huge mausoleum made from imported Italian marble and the entrance has a bronze casting of an AK-47 and next to it a sculpture of Santa Muerte (Holy Death), the female skeletal figure dressed in a long robe. Several men on weekends come to La Sombra's tomb and play narco ballads and drink shots of tequila in his honor.

Yet, he is just as dead as the lowliest peasant buried in a plain wooden box.

Almost a year passes and Romero's attorney Fernandez comes to see him. He is excited and can barely contain himself.

He whispers, "Buenas noticias, el túnel está directamente debajo de usted. En un día harán un agujero para su escape. Una vez que salga del túnel, usted será conducido a un rancho cercano, donde tenemos uno de sus aviones listos para salir. Usted debe estar listo porque no vamos a tener un montón de tiempo." (Good news, the tunnel is directly below you. In one day, they will make a hole in your cell for your escape. Once you exit the tunnel, you will be driven to a nearby ranch where we have one of your planes ready to take you away from the area. You must be ready because we will not have a lot of time.)

"Perfecto, no puedo soportar estar encerrado por más tiempo. Estoy volviendo me loco. Asegurarse de que todo está arreglado con los sobornos. No podemos tener cualquier problemas. Tengo confianza en ti." (Perfect, I cannot stand being locked up any longer. It's driving me crazy. Make sure everything is arranged with the bribes. We can't have anything go wrong. I trust you.)

Fernandez replies, "No se preocupe! Todo ha sido arreglado. Hemos pagado más de tres millones de dólares en sobornos para asegurarse de que nada va mal. El dinero y la intimidación funcionan mucho mejor que las balas." (Do not worry! Everything has been arranged. We have paid more than three million dollars in bribes to make sure nothing goes wrong. Money and intimidation are better than bullets.)

"Ya hecho arreglos con Pablo Martinez, el comandante del Bloque Sur de las FARC de proporcionarme protección mientras estoy en Colombia. Puedo coordinar el movimiento de cocaína procedente de Colombia, directamente con él y sus hombres. Sabe usted que la FARC controla de sesenta a setenta por ciento de la cocaína en el país? En virtud de su bloque, hay unos dieciocho frentes por lo que es uno de los más poderosos de los siete bloques. El Bloque Sur se encuentra junto a la frontera con Ecuador y Perú. Opera en Caquetá, Huila, Putumayo, y partes de Cauca." (I've already made arrangements with Pablo Martinez, the commander of the FARC's Southern Bloc to provide me with protection while I'm in Colombia. I can coordinate the movement of cocaine from Colombia directly with him and his men. Do you know that the FARC controls sixty to seventy percent of the cocaine in the country? Under his command are about eighteen fronts making it one of the most powerful of the seven FARC blocs. It operates close to the border with Ecuador and Peru. It includes the departments (states) of Caqueta, Huila, Putumayo, and parts of Cauca.)

Fernandez smirks, "Albino, le deseo buena suerte mañana. Vamos a estar en contacto mientras se encuentra en Colombia y yo podemos mantenerlo informado de las cosas aquí. Cuídate." (Albino, I wish you good luck tomorrow. We'll be in touch while you're in Colombia and I can keep you informed of things here. Take care.)

Romero, the following afternoon, sits on his stone hard bed and is startled by thunderous pounding on the floor near his bed. Inmates in other nearby cells scream their complaints of the crashing sounds. The hammering and yells of insults and profanity continue for fifteen minutes. No guards appear. They dare not show up. The noise abruptly stops and an eerie silence envelops the entire cellblock. Romero has disappeared. He squeezes through a small hole and quickly climbs down a wooden ladder into the dimly lit tunnel.

The air is stale. He jumps into a cart used to haul dirt out of the tunnel. It's hooked up to a modified motorcycle on a track and he is whisked away. They are moving so fast; the cart and motorcycle almost turn over. Romero is breathing hard and he is sweating from the thin dusty air. He arrives at the end of the tunnel and climbs a ladder to freedom. He smiles and takes a deep breath of fresh air. His lungs are revived. No time to waste. Romero jumps into a late model brown sedan and speeds away from the area. By the time the alarm is sounded, Romero is safely in the air headed south towards Colombia.

All hell breaks loose at La Palma when authorities learn of Romero's spectacular escape. The military and federal police immediately set up roadblocks within a ten-mile radius. It is too late. Prison officials waited an hour to report the escape. Ventura is put in charge of the investigation and he focuses on the prison staff. He is a tough interrogator and uses torture if needed. Within hours, several of the prison guards have confessed and point the finger at the warden and almost every official at the prison.

Ventura determines that numerous prison policies have been blatantly violated. The procedure of cell rotation every month didn't happen with Romero. He was in the same ground level cell during the entire time of his incarceration. Also, sensors were turned off that would have detected underground tunnel construction. Officials ignored the loud pounding when the tunnel diggers were punching a hole into Romero's cell. Romero's tracking bracelet was also removed on the day of escape. Prison guards at the control center who monitored the surveillance cameras in Romero's cell didn't report his disappearance for an hour.

The warden and twenty-five other officials are arrested and quickly sent to prison for ten years. Most of them are relieved they are still among the living and breathing. They survive death, but lose their freedom. When the game is over, the king and the pawn go back into the same box.

CHAPTER 11

The Capture

Villa is busy and has little time for a social life. One evening, however, he stops at a small, cozy bar, which is decorated with old photos of the Mexican Revolution. The walls are painted in a subtle red color. It is dimly lit and the indirect lighting from behind the bar is the only source of illumination. He sits on a tall wooden stool at the bar and orders a frozen margarita made with El Patron tequila.

He reflects on the events of the past couple of years and the savage, brutal violence he has witnessed much too frequently. He is gloomy, thinking of the many friends he has lost in the barbaric struggle against illegal drugs. He sips the strong margarita and it begins to have a calming effect on him. He notices a beautiful woman in her early thirties walk in wearing a short, black dress with red high heels, which match her fiery red hair. She sits two barstools away and orders a glass of house merlot. Villa discretely tells the bartender he will pick up her bill. He nods his head and smiles.

Villa starts the conversation, "Buenas tardes… Como estas?" (Good afternoon… How are you?)

She smiles, "Estoy bien. Es usted de la Ciudad de México? Lo siento, debo presentarme primero. Mi nombre es Taylor Mendoza y trabajo en un banco cercano. Cuál es su nombre?" (I'm fine. Are you from Mexico City? Sorry, I should introduce myself first. My name is Taylor Mendoza and I work at a nearby bank. What is your name?)

"Mi nombre es Miguel Villa y para responder a su pregunta, yo no soy de la Ciudad de México. Nací y crecí en Nuevo México." (My name is Miguel Villa and to answer your question, I am not from Mexico City. I was born and raised in New Mexico.)

She raises her glass, "Para la salud y la felicidad. Por cierto, qué haces en nuestra preciosa, pero contaminada ciudad? Debe estar cansado del tráfico terrible que tenemos." (To health and happiness. By the way, what are you doing in our beautiful, but contaminated city? You must be tired of the terrible traffic we have?)

Villa replies, "Para la salud y la felicidad! Tengo que decir que estoy acostumbrado al tráfico pesado y la contaminación. Tiene su problemas, pero sigue siendo una de las ciudades más bellas del mundo. Me encanta la cultura y su historia." (To health and happiness! I have to say that I'm used to heavy traffic and pollution. It has its problems, but it remains one of the most beautiful cities in the world. I love the culture and history.)

Taylor asks, "Donde trabajas? Lo que supongo que es algún lugar cerca? (Where do you work? I guess it is somewhere nearby?)

"Yo trabajo en la embajada," he answers. (I work at the embassy.)

Villa never told strangers he worked for the DEA and Taylor is no exception. They chat for an hour and before leaving she gives Villa her business card so they can get together for lunch. When the bartender tells her Villa paid her check, she gives Villa a kiss, imprinting her lips in red on his cheek. Villa looks at the card and sees Banco Azteca in large letters. It is located in the Zona Rosa (The Pink Zone) five blocks from the embassy.

The following morning, Villa checks the bank and Taylor Mendoza through the DEA's criminal database. He finds an obscure reference to the bank in an old investigative report. It says, "Source indicates that Banco Azteca may be involved in money laundering." The source was deactivated when he later died of natural causes. Nothing is found on Mendoza.

Villa calls Ventura and meets him for lunch near the bank. He tells him about his chance encounter with Mendoza and that he conducted background checks on her and the bank. Villa says he has a hunch and wants to do some further inquiries. They decide to have two of Ventura's men conduct surveillance on the bank for several days. After four days, the men report unusual activity at the bank. They say that the same group of five men and three women go to the bank every day, sometimes two or three times. They always carry either boxes or duffel bags inside.

One of Ventura's men visits the bank, but whatever business they are doing is being done behind closed doors in the executive offices. Taking it to the next level, Villa and Ventura decide to begin intercepting the banks phones, including Mendoza's.

They check with the local Camara de Commercio (Chamber of Commerce) and determine that the president of Banco Azteca is Emilio Vargas. Ventura finds out he did three years in a Mexican prison for fraud ten years ago. It is becoming more and more interesting. The wire intercepts begin to yield results.

Vargas receives a call from someone named El Negro who says, "Emilio, vas a recibir un millón de dólares por la tarde y necesitamos que lo transfiere a Industrias Titan en Panamá. Necesitamos que llame a su contacto para establecer otra empresa para nosotros allí." (Emilio, you will receive one million dollars in the afternoon and we need you to transfer it to Titan Industries in Panama. We need you to call your contact to establish another company for us there.)

Vargas replies, "Creo que es una buena idea para que se establezca otra compañía offshore para usted. Es necesario difundir el dinero en otras empresas que hacen que sea difícil para cualquier persona para rastrearlo. Voy a llamar a Trujillo para que pueda preparar los documentos. Él está en el proceso de mover su bufete de abogados a otro edificio." (I think it's a good idea to establish another offshore company. You need to spread the money into other companies to make it difficult for anyone to trace it. I'll call Trujillo so he can prepare the documents. He is in the process of moving his law firm to another building.)

El Negro says, "Eso está bien. Pregúntale si ya ha pagado los cinco millones de dólares para el rancho que queremos en La Chorrera. Es posible que desea comprar otro, pero lo dejamos saber más tarde." (That's fine. Ask him if he has already paid the five million dollars for the ranch we want in La Chorrera. We may want to buy another, but will let him know later.)

"Él ya ha pagado por el rancho y los documentos han sido enviados aquí. Y les daré a usted cuando llegan. Si decide comprar otro rancho dejarme saber qué sociedad offshore que desea utilizar. Ahora tiene veinte de ellos. Cuando se envía el millón de dólares asegurarse de que los dan a Taylor," answers Vargas. (He has already paid for the ranch and the documents have been sent here. I will give them to you when they arrive. If you decide to buy another ranch let me know what offshore company to use. You now have twenty of them. When you send the million dollars ensure that they give it to Taylor.)

El Negro says, "Gracias a Dios por companias offshore. No hay mejor forma de lavar dinero de la droga. Esto hace que sea difícil para cualquier persona de averiguar quién posee realmente las empresas o el dinero. Te llamaré pronto." (Thank God for offshore companies. There is no better way to launder drug money. This makes it difficult for anyone to find out who actually owns the companies or money. I'll call you soon.)

Ventura and Villa look at each other incredulously at El Negro's last comment and think how stupid of him to make such an incriminating statement. El Negro has just sealed the fate of his operation. Villa is fully aware of offshore corporations and their primary objective of anonymity. Secrecy can be a good thing or a bad thing because criminals can use it to hide or legitimize drug money. It can be exploited into a shell game where one company owns another one and then a third one and so on. They are like the famous Russian Matryoshka dolls, which hides a smaller one and that one hides yet another smaller one. There are law firms, which create offshore companies for a fee and for additional money will use their clerks to act as the president, secretary, and treasurer of the offshore corporation. They are called nominee directors, but they take their orders from the real owners. The corporations can be used to open bank accounts or purchase property. These transactions are not all illegal since legitimate businessmen use them to hide their identity when buying property to avoid the hiking up of prices by the owners. In this case, which involves Banco Azteca, it is clearly to launder drug money and criminal in nature.

In the afternoon, Ventura and Villa, with a large team of agents watch the entrance of Banco Azteca. Suddenly, a white Nissan SUV pulls up in front. Two men get down and remove two large duffel bags. The agents move in, guns drawn, and point them at the two men. They are startled by the show of guns and don't know if it is a robbery or they are being arrested. They are thrown down hard on the pavement and their hands are handcuffed behind their backs. Ventura and Villa move rapidly into the bank. They order everyone out of the building and then find Taylor and Vargas in an opulent office in the back.

Vargas yells, "Quien diablos son ustedes? Estos son oficinas privadas y tienen nada que hacer aquí. Salen de aquí antes de que llame a la policía." (Who the hell are you? These are private offices and you have nothing to do here. Get out of here before I call the police.)

Ventura laughs, "No se moleste, somos la policía. Ponte de pie y darse la vuelta, los dos están bajo arresto." (Do not bother! We are the police. Stand up and turn around, the two of you are under arrest.)

Taylor looks at Villa and smiles. In a soft voice she says, "Sólo mi suerte. Debería haber sabido. Oh, bueno, supongo que no podemos comer juntos." (Just my luck. I should have known. Oh, well, I guess we can't eat together.)

Villa believes his job makes it near impossible to have a social life, especially if you are totally committed to its mission. Regardless, it is not a lonely life because of the unparalleled adventure and the danger. Your family becomes those who share life with you, like Ventura.

Vargas sings like a canary when interrogated by Ventura. He identifies El Negro as Jairo Velasquez, one of the top money launderers for the Blood Alliance Cartel. Later that afternoon, based on information provided by Vargas, a raid is conducted at Room 122 of the hotel Toluca in the downtown area of Mexico City. Villa and Ventura kick down the door and find Velasquez in bed with a prostitute.

He screams, "No me mates! No me mates! Les puedo dar un montón de dinero. Por favor, tengo una familia." (Do not kill me! Do not kill me! I can give you a lot of money. Please, I have a family.)

Ventura frowns and says, "Cállate, maldito payaso. No somos sicarios. Estamos aquí para arrestarlo por lavado de dinero para el Cartel Alianza de Sangre. Ponga sus manos en el aire, donde pueda verlas." (Shut up, damn clown. We are not killers and are here to arrest you for laundering money for the Blood Alliance Cartel. Put your hands in the air where I can see them.)

As swift as a rattlesnake, Velasquez pulls out a Colt .45 from underneath the covers and yells, "Chingen a su madre!" (Fuck your mother!) He pulls the trigger. The loud blast causes the prostitute to scream at the top of her lungs. A bullet hits the door between Villa and Ventura who then return fire at the same time. Within seconds it is all over and Velasquez is riddled with six bullets. Blood begins to pour from his mouth, with a loud gurgling sound, choking him to death. The white sheets are quickly soaked in dark, red blood. The naked prostitute with disheveled hair is now screaming even louder. She is told to dress and leave the premises.

Quickly she reaches into Velasquez's wallet on the dresser and pulls out several large bills and says, "Mi servicio, como ustedes saben, no es gratis. No me gustó el bastardo barato de todos modos. Adiós." (My services, as you know, are not free. I didn't like the cheap bastard anyway. Goodbye.) She sashays out in her six-inch spike heels and leopard skin miniskirt with a matching purse.

It takes days to go through the voluminous records in the bank, which reveal that hundreds of millions of dollars have gone through the financial institution to different offshore banks in Panama. Trujillo is identified as Anselmo Trujillo, a crooked attorney in Panama City, with one sole client, the Blood Alliance Cartel. He is arrested, without incident, in Panama by the local authorities and the DEA. A search of his office results in the seizure of massive amounts of evidence. He has laundered over two billion dollars for the cartel in less than three years, primarily by investing in businesses and also the purchase of hundreds of properties. The Panamanian government moves quickly and seizes enough assets to pay for more than half of its national debt.

Five miles north of Los Mochis, a road crew of seven men in three Ford trucks pull up and remove a large metal culvert from the back of one of the trucks. Two of the men begin to divert traffic along the shoulders of the two lane road. After using jackhammers to break up the asphalt, five of the men begin to dig out a trench across both lanes of the road. When it is deep enough, they put the culvert in and begin to cover it with dirt. They work hard and fast. It is a hot day and they are in a hurry to leave the area. The people driving by are very impressed because they have never seen a road crew work so hard.

The men get back into their trucks and drive away one behind the other in a cloud of dust. As the sun begins to set, a convoy of three SUVs approaches the area. When they are directly over the newly installed culvert a massive explosion rocks the immediate area and lifts all three vehicles, along with tons of dirt, high into the air. When they start their descent back to earth all of them catch on fire and are quickly consumed in flames. The fifteen men in the SUV's are dead and within minutes totally incinerated. One of them is Atenco, the undisputed head of the Blood Alliance Cartel.

From a distance, Lisa sits in a black Land Rover with four of her bodyguards. She takes the remote control device and throws it out the window.

Lisa tells the driver, "Vamonos" (Let's go) and they take one last look at the burning inferno and then begin their drive back to Culiacan. Lisa is silent and thinks of all the murder and mayhem. She comes to the conclusion that drug traffickers such as her, always carry a death certificate with their names on it and it is only a matter of time when it becomes a reality. Lisa knows she and everyone who deals in drugs face death every second of the day. Santa Muerte follows one step behind. The good Saint is very unforgiving and waits patiently to snatch their dark souls. Santa Muerte has now taken those of Atenco and his thugs. Now, her eyes turn toward Lisa and the wait begins again.

One afternoon, Villa gets a call at the embassy. The man on the line identifies himself as Don Juan and says it is urgent that he meets with a DEA agent. He is reluctant to discuss the matter over the telephone and is very cautious in the words he uses. Villa makes arrangements to meet him in an hour at Sanborn's restaurant close to the embassy. Don Juan says he is wearing a red shirt and blue jeans. Villa then calls Ventura to join him. Fortunately, Ventura is in the area and begins to drive there.

Both Villa and Ventura arrive early and order a cold glass of cold watermelon juice. Suddenly, they see a tall man with a large handlebar mustache, short dark hair, and large ears like a bat enter the restaurant. Villa motions him over with a wave of his hand. As he approaches, Villa notices his eyes are like those of a shark, emotionless and cold.

Villa asks, "Don Juan?"

"Sí, pero eso no es mi verdadero nombre. Soy Federico Solís. Quiero darle un poco de información. He estado trabajando para el Cártel del Norte durante aproximadamente un año. Soy parte de un equipo que es responsable de la descarga de los submarinos cargados de cocaína procedente de Colombia, cerca de la costa caribeña de México. La última vez sólo me pagaron la mitad de lo que me deben y se niegan a pagarme el resto. La próxima semana otro submarino está llegando con ocho toneladas de cocaína. Voy a ayudarte porque nadie chinga conmigo y se escapa," says Solís. (Yes, but that's not my real name. I'm Federico Solís. I want to give you some information. I have been working for the Cartel of the North for about a year. I am part of a team that is responsible for the offloading of submarines transporting cocaine from Colombia to Mexico's Caribbean coast. The last operation, I was only paid half of what they owed me and they refuse to pay the rest. Next week another submarine is coming with eight tons of cocaine. I am going to help you because no one fucks me and gets away with it.)

Villa asks, "Quién es el que esta enviando la cocaína de Colombia? Cuándo y dónde llegará?" (Who is sending cocaine from Colombia? When and where will it arrive?)

Solis says, "El submarino llegará el próximo martes, cerca de la isla de Cozumel frente a la costa oriental de la península de Yucatán. Las coordenadas son veinte grados, veintiocho minutos al norte y ochenta y seis grados, cincuenta y ocho minutos al oeste. Nos reuniremos a las cinco de la tarde. Nos estaremos comunicando en la frecuencia HF 138.7. La clave del submarino es delfín y la nuestra es halcón. La cocaína se envia de Albino Romero que se esconde en Colombia y está protegido por las FARC." (The submarine will arrive next Tuesday, near the island of Cozumel, off the east coast of the Yucatan Peninsula. The coordinates are twenty degrees, twenty-eight minutes north and eighty-six degrees, fifty-eight minutes west. We will rendezvous at about five in the afternoon. We will be communicating on HF frequency 138.7. The call sign for the submarine is dolphin and ours is hawk. The cocaine is being sent by Albino Romero who is hiding in Colombia and working with the FARC.)

"Qué tipo de barcos está usando para recoger la cocaína y que sabes acerca del submarino?" asks Villa. (What kind of boats are you using to pick up the cocaine and what do you know about the submarine?)

Solis replies, "Utilizamos un Hatteras con el nombre la Tormenta de Nieve, que es ochenta y seis pies de largo y tiene una velocidad máxima de diez ocho kilómetros por

hora. Está pintado de color blanco y tiene sofisticados equipos de radar y de comunicaciones. El submarino es más de
cuarenta pies de largo y puede viajar más de tres mil kilometros. Se puede fácilmente llevar diez toneladas de cocaína.
Está hecho de fibra de vidrio y por lo tanto no puede ser de-
tectado por el radar o sonar. Está propulsado por un motor
diesel de doscientos sesenta KW y normalmente tiene una
tripulación de tres. Se desplaza a unos treinta pies bajo la
superficie del agua." (We use a Hatteras named Snow Storm,
which is eighty-six feet long and has a top speed of eighteen
kilometers per hour. It is painted white and has sophisticated
radar and communications systems. The submarine is over
forty feet long and can travel more than three thousand kilometers. It can easily carry ten tons of cocaine. It is made of
fiberglass and therefore cannot be detected by radar or sonar.
It is powered by a two hundred and sixty KW diesel engine
and normally has a crew of three. It travels about thirty feet
below the surface of the water.)

Villa asks, "Cuánto tiempo se tarda en descargar ocho toneladas de cocaína desde el submarino?" (How long does it
take to download the eight tons of cocaine from the submarine?)

"Se tarda mas de dos horas, ya que es difícil de descargar
la cocaína del submarino. Ustedes tendrán un montón de
tiempo para hacer su operación. Voy a estar en el Hatteras y
les voy a dar una señal en la frecuencia HF 140.5 diciendo
que el fiesta ha comenzado. Me dejan escapar después.
Acuerdo?" (It takes more than two hours, because it is difficult and very labor intensive to unload. You will have plenty
of time to do your operation. I'll be on the Hatteras and I will
send you a signal on HF frequency 140.5 saying that the
party has begun. You will let me escape later. Agree?)

Ventura tells Solis, "Vamos a dejarte escapar, si no nos chingas. Si lo hace, entonces usted es un hombre muerto caminando. Estamos claros?" (We will let you escape, as long as you don't fuck us. If you do, then you are a dead man walking. Are we clear?)

"No estoy aquí para jugar juegos. Mi único propósito es vengarse de los hijos de puta que me chingaron con el dinero que me debían," says Solis (I'm not here to play games. My sole purpose is revenge on the sons of whores who fucked me with the money they owed me.)

Villa gives Solis his cell number and takes his so they can have constant contact, especially if things change. Solis shakes hands with Ventura and Villa and quietly leaves the restaurant avoiding eye contact with everyone.

Ventura asks Villa how much the traffickers pay to build a narco-sub? Villa explains the cost is between two and four million dollars, but one good load easily covers the expense twenty times over. Villa reminisces when the traffickers initially used speedboats, then later shifted to semi-submersibles. The semi-submersibles travel slightly underwater, but the cockpit and exhaust pipes can be seen sticking several feet above the water. Ever adaptable, the traffickers begin to use narco-subs, making their smuggling ventures much more successful. Villa also knows they are equipped with advanced radar, GPS, and sophisticated technology. The operation will be no easy task and the timing has to be very precise.

The next day, Ventura and Villa meet with trusted members of the Mexican navy and air force to plan the operation. The session is dynamic and heats up as everyone has different plans and ideas, but after a long, heavy lunch things become more civilized and focused. It is decided that the air force will forward deploy two helicopters, a UH-60 Black Hawk with side door mounted .50 caliber machine guns and a light 500 MD Defender. The Defender is an anti-submarine helicopter with search radar and the capability to carry lightweight aerial torpedoes. On Monday, the day prior to the arrival of the narco-sub the helicopters and crews will be placed in an isolated area south of San Benito, Cozumel.

The navy will also position two of its Polaris Interceptor boats near the operational site. The Polaris Interceptors have speeds of fifty knots per hour and are equipped with computerized navigational systems. They also have mounted .50 caliber machine guns. Ventura and Villa will be in the Black Hawk. They will monitor the frequency Solis will use to notify them the offload of the cocaine from the sub is underway.

On Sunday, Villa receives a call on his cell phone from Solis. He says, "Todo está listo para este martes en el lugar y el tiempo que te di. Yo te daré la señal como estaba previsto. Buena suerte." (Everything is set for Tuesday at the place and time I gave you. I will give the signal as planned. Good luck.)

The next day, all the boats, helicopters and men move into position and wait. The hours drift by ever so slowly. Everyone is impatient for the action to begin. This is where their training and experience will be crucial to the execution of the operational plan. All of the agencies involved have to be in sync like a well-oiled machine. Fate will be unkind if just one agency falters in its responsibilities.

The following day, they eat bland military meals-ready-to-eat. When going into armed conflict, optimum energy levels are a must. A final briefing is given and the equipment and weapons are checked one last time. Everyone is prepared and they know they have to work closely together and watch each other's backs.

At about six in the afternoon, the signal from Solis comes over the radio. Seconds later, the whine of helicopter engines revving up is deafening. Radio chatter crackles between the helicopters and the naval boats. The helicopters lift a few feet of the ground and hover there for a few seconds. More radio chatter and then they pull rapidly upwards into the sky filled with thick clouds. Two marines grab the heavy machine guns on each door and loudly crank an armor-piercing bullet into each chamber. In twenty minutes, the helicopters make their approach and can see a large black submarine alongside the Hatteras. Two men on the submarine begin to fire at the helicopters with AK-47's. It is too late as the Defender helicopter, like a dragonfly, swoops low and launches a small torpedo at the broadside of the sub. The men see it coming and with wild screams plunge into the cold, blue water. The torpedo slams into the sub with a massive explosion sending smoke and fire into the tropical sky. Debris rains down from the air and fills the water where several men are bobbing up and down. The Hatteras begins to move away and now the Black Hawk moves over it and the repetitive thunder of the .50 caliber machine guns is numbing to the ears.

Villa sees the bullets stitching across the water as they speed toward the inboard motors of the boat. They quickly find their mark splintering wood and blowing up the engines. The boat lies dead in the water and several men appear on deck holding their hands in the air as the Polaris Interceptors approach. The Mexican navy fishes four men out of the water and arrests seven others on the Hatteras. Five tons of cocaine is seized on the Hatteras. Three tons were still onboard the sub when it went up in flames and quickly sank into the deep water. Solis is discretely released without the other defendants being aware and disappears never to be heard from again.

Later Villa and Ventura interrogate the captain of the sub, Jacobo Candelaria. He is a hardened sea veteran who admits smuggling close to a hundred tons of cocaine each year for the past eight years. He is short and fat with a face that looks like leather.

When asked about Romero, he says, "Romero se encuentra en el sur de Colombia, en el departamento de Putumayo. Él está bajo la protección de la Primer Frente del Bloque Sur de las FARC. El comandante del Bloque Sur, Pablo Martínez, es un amigo cercano de el. El comandante de la Primer Frente es Santiago Lujan. Trabajan en estrecha colaboración, grandes cargamentos de droga." (Romero is located in southern Colombia, in the department (state) of Putumayo. He is under the protection of the First Front of the FARC's powerful Southern Bloc. The commander of the Southern Bloc, Pablo Martinez, is a close friend of his. The commander of the First Front is Santiago Lujan. Both are experienced and respected leaders. They collaborate closely on large drug shipments.)

Villa asks, "Romero se esconde en qué parte de Putomayo? Qué más puede decirnos de él? (Romero hides in what part of Putumayo? What else can you tell us about him?)

"Romero está en el campo principal de la Primera Frente y se encuentra justo en el punto donde los departamentos Colombianos de Putumayo y Amazonas se reúnen con Perú. También sé que Martínez, el comandante del bloque, se comunica con sus ocho comandantes de frentes dos veces al día a través de la radio de onda corta. Para aislar a sí mismo, Martínez se basa en su operador de radio llamado Omar para enviar directivas y mensajes. Los operadores de radio para los distintos frentes a continuación, pasar los mensajes a sus comandantes y luego responden a Omar. Sé que durante la conferencia telefónica inicial, Omar le dirá a los diferentes operadores de radio para cambiar a diferentes frecuencias y luego hablar con ellos por separado por razones de seguridad. En otras palabras, ellos compartimentos sus mensajes de radio." (Romero is in the main camp of the First Front, which is right at the point where the Colombian departments of Putumayo and Amazonas meet with Peru. I also know that Martinez, commander of the bloc, communicates with his eight front commanders twice daily via shortwave radio. Martinez uses his radio operator named Omar to send directives and messages. The radio operators for the different fronts pass the messages to their commanders and then report back to Omar. I know that during the initial conference call, Omar will tell the different radio operators to switch to different frequencies and then talk to them separately for security reasons. In other words, they compartmentalize their radio messages.)

Villa, after interrogating Candelaria, calls his great friend, General Gallego in Colombia to ask for his help.

The General listens intently and says, "Usted y Ventura tienen que viajar a Bogotá para que podamos planear una operación para capturar Romero. No va a ser fácil, ya que el Bloque Sur de las FARC es muy fuerte y el Primer Frente es uno de los más grandes bajo el Bloque Sur y sin duda el más violento. Nuestra operación tiene que ser perfecto, absolutamente sin errores." (You and Ventura have to travel to Bogota so we can plan an operation to capture Romero. It will not be easy as the Southern Bloc of the FARC is very strong. The First Front is one of the largest under the Southern Bloc and certainly the most violent. Our operation has to be perfect, absolutely without errors.)

"Está bien, mi hermano! Vamos a tomar un vuelo a Bogotá en dos días. Le llamaré con la información de vuelo. Será bueno volver a verte. Mis mejores deseos para su familia." (Okay, my brother! We will take a flight to Bogota in two days. I'll call you with the flight information. It will be good to see you again. Best wishes to your family.)

Two days later, Ventura and Villa arrive at the El Dorado airport in Bogota. They only have carry-on-bags and walk past several gates and rows of elegant restaurants. They submit their immigration forms and clear customs without a search.

Waiting outside is General Gallego and ten of his men. He and Villa give each other a hug and then Villa introduces Ventura. They shake hands and start to walk briskly out of the terminal to a couple of armored cars waiting outside. On the way to the hotel, the men make small talk about work and some of the most interesting operations they have worked on in their respective countries.

They finally arrive at the W. Bogota Hotel located in the commercial district. Villa and Ventura walk through the colorful lobby that is beautifully decorated with tasteful art. Villa sees what appears to be a Botero painting and wonders if it is an original. After checking in, they take the elevator to the fourth floor and leave their bags in their small rooms. Minutes later, they meet with General Gallego in one of the funky bars downstairs and have some *Aguardiente*. Villa is not a fan of the licorice-flavored liquor, but is glad to enjoy a few toasts with his close friends. The General is wearing his immaculate, green uniform, which is so full of medals that there is no room for anymore. After quickly catching up on each other's lives, successes, and defeats, they get down to business.

General Gallego says, "Estoy familiarizado con el protocolo de comunicación del Bloque Sur de las FARC y he estado involucrado en la escucha de ellos por mucho tiempo. Los dos radio operadores principals son Omar y Diablo. También sé donde se encuentra el Primer Frente. Está fuertemente fortificado con los rebeldes. Nuestro ejército les ha bombardeado y llevado a cabo ataques terrestres, pero no ha tenido grandes resultados, ya que huyen rápidamente a través de la frontera con Perú." (I am familiar with the communication protocol of the FARC's Southern Bloc and have been involved in monitoring them for a long time. The two primary radio operators are known as Omar and Diablo. I also know where the First Front is located. The rebels heavily fortify the area with several rings of security and trenches. Our army has bombed them and carried out ground attacks, but has not had great results as they quickly flee across the border into Peru.)

Villa responds, "Bueno, necesitamos una estrategia muy innovadora para capturar a Romero. Sólo podemos tener una oportunidad ya que las FARC le puede trasladar a otro lugar. Podrían pasar años antes de que lo localizamos otra vez." (Well, we need an innovative strategy to capture Romero. We may only have one chance because the FARC can move him somewhere else. It could be years before we locate him again.)

All three men agree that a great strategy is needed to capture Romero. Long into the night, they discuss different tactics and quickly discard them as unrealistic. Tired and frustrated, they call it a day. They will resume the following day when they are rested and can think more clearly.

Villa goes to his room and wants to jump into the king size bed with oversized pillows, but decides to take a long hot shower. The spray of hot water is soothing and relaxes him. He is stressed and tired. His mind begins to ponder about the fine line between good and evil. He is repulsed at the terrible things people are willing to do for money, but is proud of the people who are committed to taking great risks to stop them. Villa dries himself with a large, soft towel and crawls into the firm bed and quickly goes into a comatose sleep.

Early the next day, Villa meets with Ventura and General Gallego to continue the intense planning. By late afternoon, they come up with a bold, but risky strategy. It will involve the exploitation and manipulation of the Southern Bloc's communications. They will wait for a lull in radio transmissions from Omar to the various front commanders then one of General Gallego's men will get on the air posing as Omar and contact Diablo, the radio operator for Lujan. To make it more realistic, several other Colombian national police officers will also get on the air posing as radio operators for the other fronts. Diablo will be told to shift to another frequency, separating him from the other radio operators by the fake Omar and then bogus messages will be sent through him to Lujan.

It is also decided the Colombian army will play a critical role by attacking the area where Martinez is known to have his headquarters just before the communications are initiated by the fake Omar. They will conduct a ground operation and also do saturation bombing of the area. It is designed to keep Martinez occupied and off the air. This is important for the ruse to work. Finally, the fake Omar will contact Diablo and tell him that Martinez wants to meet personally with Romero and Lujan to discuss the logistics on a multi-ton cocaine smuggling venture. He will also say that a helicopter will be sent to pick them up. Villa, Ventura, and General Gallego are confident that Lujan will comply with the order he believes is from Martinez. Martinez is one of the top commanders in the FARC and his orders are executed unconditionally. To do otherwise means execution by a firing squad.

For several days, General Gallegos's men listen to the FARC's transmissions to learn the accents and words used by Omar and the other radio operators of the different fronts. Phase one of the operation begins early Saturday in the morning as five thousand army troops in green camouflage uniforms swarm the area south of Solono, Caqueta. They have drawn a circle on a map and based on prior intelligence know that Martinez's headquarters is located within a five-mile radius.

Ahead of the military troops are aircraft dropping bombs forcing the FARC to run and disperse like cockroaches. Many of the rebels are killed in the initial assault and Martinez flees into the jungle and is now on the run as chaos and pandemonium overcome his troops. The loud explosions rip through the jungle canopy and crater the ground all around them. They scatter in different directions, including Omar who panics and runs. He separates from Martinez leaving him without communication.

For five days, Martinez can't contact the fronts under his command as he wanders through the jungle with some of his troops. Meantime, the fake Omar has a conference call with the radio operators of the different front commanders and issues false orders. He then directs Diablo onto a different frequency and tells him that Martinez wants to immediately meet with Lujan and Romero to plan a multi-ton cocaine venture with them. He tells Diablo that a UH-1H helicopter from a Peruvian military sympathizer will be sent to transport them to Martinez. He is given coordinates, close to the first front, where the rendezvous will take place the next day.

An hour later, Diablo contacts the fake Omar and tells him that Romero and Lujan will be at the site. Villa, Ventura, and General Gallego now pray that nothing goes wrong. They ready an old UH-1H helicopter painted green and Peruvian military emblems are pasted on. The three men, representing three countries, will travel in the helicopter wearing seized FARC uniforms.

The next morning, a gloomy, overcast day infested with mosquitos, they board the decrepit helicopter, which is barely airworthy and has no side doors. Villa feels claustrophobic in the tight FARC uniform and tightens his muscles trying to stretch it. It doesn't work. The helicopter lifts high in the air and begins to fly over the thick, deep green canopy of trees and vegetation. Villa can see why it is difficult to locate rebel camps even from the air. As the helicopter adjusts its trajectory and makes several sharps turns, the men grab on to ropes hanging over their heads. The helicopter doesn't even have seatbelts. The mountain range begins to thin out and they approach flatter surfaces.

One of the pilots comes on the radio, "Estamos casi allí y comenzará a descender ahora. Que Dios nos bendiga a todos." (We're almost there and we will begin to descend now. May God bless us all.)

Villa gives him a thumbs-up and smiles. The men quickly check their weapons and make sure they are ready to go at a moment's notice. They take a deep breath knowing they are going literally into the den of the wolf. The helicopter does a quick low-level pass over the rendezvous site. They see nothing and on the second pass the helicopter hovers a hundred feet above the ground and slowly touches down softly.

A few seconds pass before they see Romero and Lujan running towards the helicopter. Both are carrying Ak-47's. They exchange greetings, but can't hear each other over the loud spinning rotors. Both men jump into the helicopter. Lujan's hair is dirty and matted. His uniform is full of caked mud. He is short and very thin. When he smiles, most of his teeth are gone and the others should be pulled out. Romero looks like he has seen better times.

When the helicopter is a few hundred feet from the ground, weapons are pulled and pointed at Romero and Lujan. They are disarmed and the look of shock doesn't leave their faces. Romero remains quiet while Lujan protests saying the FARC is negotiating a peace treaty with the government.

General Gallego says, "La FARC nunca ha tenido la intención de firmar un tratado de paz. Vete al infierno!" (The FARC has never had any intention of signing a peace treaty. Go to hell!)

Suddenly, Romero yells, "Es hora de morir," (It's time to die) and jumps out of the helicopter. He tumbles through the air and then ploughs head first into the ground below. Lujan's eyes are wide open in disbelief.

He says, "Que Dios lo bendiga. Era un buen amigo de las FARC." (May God bless him. He was a good friend of the FARC.)

252 Michael S. Vigil

Villa, Ventura, and General Gallego know their struggle is one that will probably never end, but they are hunters of the most dangerous predators on earth.

Ernest Hemingway said,

"There is no hunting like the hunting of man, and those who have hunted armed men long enough and liked it, never care for anything else thereafter."

The three men lean slowly back into their seats and envision the next hunt. All of them look at each other and smile.

ABOUT THE AUTHOR

Michael S. Vigil, born and raised in New Mexico, earned his degree in Criminology at New Mexico State University where he graduated with Honors. He later joined the Drug Enforcement Administration and became one of its most highly decorated agents. He served in thirteen foreign and domestic posts and rose through the ranks to the highest level of the Senior Executive Service.

Mr. Vigil has received numerous awards during his elite career such as Law Enforcement's most prestigious recognition: The National Association of Police Organization's (NAPO) Top Cop Award. Many foreign governments have honored Mr. Vigil for his extraordinary service in the violent struggle against transnational organized crime. He was made an honorary General by the country of Afghanistan and China bestowed him with the "Key to the City" of Shanghai. The President of the Dominican Republic also presented him with an Admiral's sword. He is mentioned in numerous books and appears on documentaries and popular television programs such as *Gangsters: America's Most Evil and Manhunt*

He is a contributor to the highly regarded Cipher Brief. His highly acclaimed memoir, *DEAL*, was released in 2014. *Metal Coffins: The Blood Alliance Cartel* is his first fiction novel and many of the scenarios are derived from his experiences as an undercover agent.

CPSIA information can be obtained
at www.ICGtesting.com
Printed in the USA
LVOW12*1424071216

516242LV00006B/63/P